A STARVING
MADNESS

A STARVING MADNESS

*Tales of hunger,
hope & healing in
psychotherapy*

Judith Ruskay Rabinor, Ph.D.

gürze books

A Starving Madness
Tales of hunger, hope & healing in psychotherapy

© 2002 by Judith Ruskay Rabinor

Gürze Books
PO Box 2238
Carlsbad, CA 92018
(760) 434-7533
www.gurze.com

Cover design by Abacus Graphics, Oceanside, CA

Library of Congress Cataloging-in-Publication Data

Rabinor, Judith Ruskay, 1942-
    A starving madness: tales of hunger, hope & healing in psychotherapy / Judith Ruskay Rabinor
        p. cm.
    Includes bibliographical references and index.
    ISBN 0-936077-41-7 (alk. paper)
    1. Eating disorders—Adjuvant treatment—Case studies.
    2. Psychotherapy—Case studies.
    3. Rabinor, Judith Ruskay, 1942- I. Title.
        RC552.E18 R33 2001
        616.85'260651—dc21   2001053186

The authors and publishers of this book intend for this publication to provide accurate information. It is sold with the understanding that it is meant to complement, not be a substitute for, professional medical and/or psychological services.

The individuals described in this book have been thoroughly disguised to preserve confidentiality.

The following poems are reprinted with permission: "Don't Change" by Anthony De Mello S.J.; "Slipping Through the Cracks" by Leslea Newman; and "Autobiography in Five Chapters" by Portia Nelson.

First Edition
3 5 7 9 0 8 6 4 2

Dedication

I dedicate this book to my grandmother, Sophie Liebowitz Ruskay (1885-1980), my sister-in-law, Shira Greenberg Ruskay (1945-1998) and my mother, Peggy Lipschutz Ruskay Neidenberg (1918-) who each, in her own way, inspired this book.

Autobiography in Five Chapters

—PORTIA NELSON

1.
I walk down the street.
There is a deep hole in the sidewalk.
I fall in.
I am lost ... I am hopeless.
          It isn't my fault.
It takes forever to find a way out.

2.
I walk down the same street.
There is a deep hole in the sidewalk.
I pretend I don't see it.
I fall in again.
I can't believe I am in the same place.
          But still, it isn't my fault.
It still takes a long time to get out.

3.
I walk down the same street.
There is a deep hole in the sidewalk.
I see it there.
I still fall in...it's a habit.
My eyes are open.
I know where I am.
It is my fault.
I get out immediately.

4.
I walk down the same street.
There is a deep hole in the sidewalk.
I walk around it.

5.
I walk down another street.

Table of Contents

Acknowledgments

This book took years to write and is an outgrowth of many relationships. First and foremost, I thank my patients whose voices fill these pages. Without their willingness to share their pain, this book could not have been written.

Over the years many people have supported my work and my writing. I would especially like to acknowledge the enormous help given to me by Lindsey Hall and Leigh Cohn, who are far more than publishers. Both of them have devoted endless support to envisioning what this book could become. Lindsey, I thank you for encouraging my writing for over a decade and for patiently supporting me in endless small and large ways during the transformation of this project from a dream to a reality. Leigh, much gratitude for the opportunity to create the column *The Therapist's Voice*, where many of the stories in this book first appeared. More thanks to Cindy Maynard, Elaine Buechler and the entire Gürze staff who contributed to this final product.

I also want to give special thanks to my editor, Barbara Aria, for handling this project with just the right touch and making my voice ring true throughout. Your perceptiveness and clarity helped keep me going even when the waters were turbulent. To my agent, Claire Gerus, thank you for your vision and devotion. To Elaine Edelman, I am grateful for your enthusiasm and inspiration when I began this book at the New School.

I am indebted to hundreds of scholars and thinkers who, over the years, have taught me about the complexity of human development, eating disorders, and psychotherapy. I am particularly grateful to the new maps of female development (now expanded to apply to males, as well) developed by Carol Gilligan, Jean Baker Miller, Judy Jordan and colleagues at the Stone Center. Special gratitude to Irene Stiver, whose generosity and support was particularly helpful early on.

A special thanks to April Benson, who introduced me to The Center for the Study of Anorexia and Bulimia, my first professional home. Deep appreciation to Judi Goldstein, who drew me into my next home, The Renfrew Center, where I was offered innumerable opportunities to develop the ideas in this book at professional trainings and presentations.

I have benefited immensely from interdisciplinary supervisors, among them Yvonne Agazarian, Daniel Araoz, Bill Davis, Jerry Gold, Don David-Lusterman, Harry Popper, and Ron Taffel, who offered me different perspectives about healing and taught me so many things about being authentic as a therapist.

To the members of my Wednesday and Thursday ongoing supervision-consultation groups, you are a source of continuous challenge and inspiration.

To Marion Bilich, Ann Kearney-Cooke and Steve Zimmer, who carefully read early drafts of a multitude of chapters, I am grateful for your support, encouragement, and the gift of friendship.

Thank you to the people in my life who read parts of this manuscript, made valuable comments, and helped in innumerable ways. Among them are Nancy Bravman, Judith Brisman, Gina Colleli, Barbara Greenspan, Carol Fogash, Gladys Fox, Susan Kornblum, Sondra Kronberg, Margo Maine, Alan Miller, Shiela Rindler, Ilana Rubenfeld, Jane Stein, Kathryn Zerbe, and Joan Zuckerberg.

I am blessed to have parents, Peggy and Everett, who valued compassion towards others; a brother, John who has been a lifelong source of support and love; and a host of extended family members who created a fertile spiritual and intellectual climate which nourished my soul.

To my children, Zach and Rachel, you have witnessed and participated in the unfolding of the ideas in this book. Thank you for being my sounding board all these years and for so enriching my life.

Finally, I want to thank my husband, Larry, who has offered me the secure base I needed to launch this work and supported me through the long and often arduous process with love, inspiration, and music.

Introduction

*S*ome years ago, a patient introduced herself to me as "a prisoner of a starving madness." Carolyn was just 19 years old and looked like a concentration camp victim. She entered therapy and within a few months, slowly began to nourish herself, first with food and eventually by developing a deeper connection with herself and others. Several years passed, and we were saying a final goodbye when I was again reminded just how mysterious the process of healing can be.

I had asked Carolyn, "When you think about your recovery, what was most helpful: Our individual sessions? Group therapy? Antidepressants?" Without a moment's hesitation, she replied that her turning point had occurred when she was leaving my office one day and happened to catch sight of my daughter's name taped to her camp trunk. I was bewildered.

"It wasn't really the trunk, it was the name, 'Rachel,'" she explained, her eyes welling up with tears. Rachel had been her grandmother's name, and would have been hers if Grandma Rachel and most of her family had not been killed in the Holocaust. Carrying with them the scars of fear, oppression, and prejudice, Carolyn's parents gave her a name that would conceal her Jewish identity. "What helped me to get better," she said, "was the fact that you named your daughter Rachel."

Carolyn's story illustrates the complexity that is at the heart of my work as a clinical psychologist specializing in the treatment of eating and body-image disorders. I have spent the past 20 years trying to understand the causes of eating disorders and what promotes healing. I have worked with hundreds of sufferers, and have lectured, conducted workshops, and trained mental health practitioners and other therapists; yet, I have never ceased to be struck by the intricate interplay of familial, cultural, biological, and psychological factors that contribute to the problem. What ignites and sustains the healing process is complex, as well. It might be the renewal of a bond with a parent or the support of a therapy group, an empathic moment with a friend or a therapist, or even something as unexpected as a spiritual connection evoked by a name on a camp trunk.

In my practice, storytelling is my primary therapeutic tool, as illustrated throughout this book. Using a variety of means, such as journal-writing, guided imagery, and EMDR, I help patients tell and understand the rich, and often painful, stories of their lives. In the process, a new narrative writes itself—one that includes our relationship. When all goes well, it is partly through the bond that forms between us that a patient begins to heal.

My approach is grounded in the pioneering work of Carol Gilligan and the Stone Center at Wellesley College. Contrary to traditional theories of psychotherapy, which emphasize separation, autonomy, and independence as the hallmarks of personal growth, this perspective states that an inner sense of connection—to oneself and others—is the central organizing feature of human life. All relationships go through periods of disconnection. However, the prolonged isolation that eating-disordered individuals suffer derails psychological growth. By developing mutually empathic and authentic relationships with my patients, I try to help them unravel the threads of their unfulfilled hungers that have become twisted into an obsession with food and weight. My ultimate goal is to help them become more resilient by teaching them how to reconnect with themselves, other people, and the universe.

The stories in *A Starving Madness*—of seven women and one man— are testimonies to the power of human connection to nourish the deepest parts of ourselves. Although names and identities have been disguised and, in some cases, composite characters created, these tales are based on the lives of real people and are representative of the multifaceted scope of eating disorders, which have become a deeply entrenched part of our cultural landscape.

Each chapter tells the tale behind one person's "I feel fat," a simple belief that can stand for a complex problem. Among them is a 15-year-old girl whose anorexia is triggered by her inability to verbalize feelings about her parents' divorce; a woman in her fifties who struggled secretly for more than a decade with bulimia; a 30-year-old compulsive eater who recovers as she remembers scenes from her childhood; and a patient who, after years of therapy and a hospitalization, quits therapy, still committed to being dangerously thin. There are also stories about college-aged women and one man who must come to grips with problems including compulsive exercise, sexual abuse, self-mutilation, and bulimia.

My experiences with clients are both the subject of this book and my motivation for writing it. Obviously, therapy affects patients, but doing therapeutic work changes the therapist, as well. Each time I open my office and heart to a new person, we establish an intimate connection that enriches both of our lives. Sufferers with eating disorders, their loved ones, and the professionals who treat them may see themselves in these tales and, I hope, be helped by them.

In addition to the readers who are drawn to *A Starving Madness* for personal or professional reasons, this book is suited for use by educators as a clinical casebook for courses on eating and body-image disorders. The reading list at the end of the book recommends specific resources to help professionals further explore these multidimensional treatment concepts and integrate them into practice.

It has been said that people only change when they're moved. Stories have the power to do that. *A Starving Madness* is not a how-to guide. I offer no simple formulas for healing. What I do offer are tales of hunger, hope, and healing to deepen your understanding, touch your heart, and inspire you on your journey.

1

Once Upon a Time

The world breaks everyone, and afterwards
some are strong in the broken places.
—ERNEST HEMINGWAY

I wonder if I will ever forget that sinking feeling in my stomach when I met Nina. It was her spindly knees that first struck me as she sat sprawled on my waiting room couch, eyes closed, sucking loudly on a straw protruding from her blue plastic water bottle. What an unforgettable sight! Dressed in running shorts and a skimpy t-shirt on an unusually chilly April afternoon, she remained still, eyes shut tight. Could those knees actually support her, I wondered? As if in response to my unasked question, she jumped up and stood before me. Face to face in an awkward silence, we stared at each other. I was the first to break the ice. "You must be Nina. I'm Doctor Judy Rabinor. Come on in."

She gathered up her belongings and followed me. In the short walk to my office, it occurred to me that I had uncharacteristically referred to myself as "Doctor." Had some intuitive radar guided me to be more formal than usual? Perhaps it was important to communicate to this malnourished young woman that we had some serious work ahead of us. The cautious way in which she curled into the deepest corner of my couch reminded me of my kitten, Floe, who, from birth, had hungered for attention but hastily backed off when it was offered. After several moments, Nina spoke up.

"I've been in therapy before, y'know. Three times. But today's my birthday, so I thought it might be a good time to start again." Was she being humorous? Sarcastic? It was too early to tell.

"How old are you today?" I asked.

"Twenty," she said. *So young, I thought, and with such tired eyes.* "Where do you want me to start?"

"Wherever you are."

"Professor Johnson—you know him?" I nodded. Jim Johnson had been my neighbor and walking partner for over a decade.

"He's the reason I'm here," she began. "He's my English professor. He thought I should see someone, and suggested you." A writing assignment she had done in Jim's English class had caught his attention.

Reaching into her knapsack, she carefully removed and opened a large manila envelope. "I might as well save you some time," she said, "and anyway, it's easier for me to read this than to start over again." Her face crumbled and she looked as though she might cry.

To start the semester, Professor Johnson had assigned what he called a "whimsical" creative writing piece. He asked the students to be imaginative and write a story entitled, "Once Upon A Time." Nina's paper concerned Professor Johnson, who asked her to meet with him after class. That was the first of a series of long talks. Eventually he suggested that she might benefit from talking to a therapist.

"How do you feel about being here?" I asked.

"Whatever," she replied with a shrug, dismissing me and her feelings with that maddeningly over-used word. She read aloud:

Once Upon a Time

Once upon a time there was a little girl who was very small. This is her story.

Once upon a time there was a very small girl. She was a sad, lonely girl who was dying for help. She had just eaten dinner yet she found herself unusually hungry. All she could think about was food.

"Mom," she said, "I'm hungry."

"Well dear, go fix yourself a bowl of ice cream and maybe you'll feel better."

That's just what the girl did. She got out a bowl and fixed herself a nice big sundae with vanilla ice cream, chocolate sauce, colored sprinkles, whipped cream, and a cherry.

Nevertheless, fifteen minutes later she found herself hungry again.

"Mom," she said, "I'm hungry."

"Well," said Mom, "maybe you could have a bowl of cereal."

"Good idea," the daughter thought, and fixed herself a big bowl of corn flakes loaded with sugar. However, this still didn't do the trick. This poor little girl was still hungry, so she went to her mom and said, "Mom, I'm still really, really hungry."

And her Mom said, "Well, go get something else to eat, and go to sleep. That will make you feel better."

So she went to the cabinet, got down another bowl, and filled it up with some more vanilla ice cream, and on top of the ice cream she sprinkled corn flakes and on top of the corn flakes, she added first some chocolate sauce, then some sugar, then some sprinkles and whipped cream, and a cherry. And then she went to bed. But she couldn't sleep.

She lay in the dark, waiting for morning.

How sad. I would think that most mothers would begin to wonder if something was wrong with their little girl.
I would hope that most mothers would address the situation instead of carelessly dismissing it like my mother did.
Never once when I said, "Mom, I'm hungry," or "Mom, I
don't want to eat," did she think of asking me why.

When she finished, she looked up at me in silence.

"Thank you," I said. "You have a gift with words." Wanting to let
her know that she had moved me, I added, "You are a born storyteller.
I am really touched that you shared this with me."

"I've been struggling with an eating disorder for years," she said.
"I've already been hospitalized once. Do you think you can help me?"

Nina's question stopped me. Even though I could tell from her
story that her earliest, most basic needs for care and contact had been
ignored, here she was asking for help again after trying three therapists. The fact that she was in my office made me think that deep
down she wanted to get well and felt optimistic that she could. I was
impressed by her courage.

"Do I think I can help you?" I echoed. "I do."

And thus began our work together.

Storytelling is the oldest healing art, and from the beginning, Nina
let me know that she had a love for it. Telling our stories adds value to
our experiences, when we describe the minutia of our daily lives. No
matter how often we have told them, each telling is a new experience
capable of unearthing buried facts and feelings, enabling us to reach
deeper personal truths. And each time we wonder and wander, we can
dream new dreams about the future. Storytelling is a ritual that lies at
the heart of psychotherapy, but sometimes one's own story can seem
hollow, and the telling of it feel canned. Perhaps that's why, as much
as she loved stories, Nina didn't feel like telling hers to me.

"Why do we have to go over all this again? I told my other therapists these same facts so many times, they no longer seem to matter," she said. "However much I talk about it all, I don't *feel* it." I wasn't surprised. Her "Once Upon a Time" tale had warned me that Nina was raised in a home where her feelings were barely acknowledged.

"Let's see what comes up if we dig down a bit. Perhaps we'll learn something if we simply sit together on the edge of the unknown," I said, for I knew that exploring the past with a witness is much different than doing it alone.

Nina did begin to open up, but talking wasn't easy for her. Then, one day, she staggered into a session bearing a huge pile of photograph albums that graphically documented the family's milestones: birthdays, graduations, and vacations. "It's easier for me to show you my family than talk about them," she explained. I was pleased that she had taken such an ingenious approach.

Nina was the second youngest of five children. She had a younger brother, Ben, two older sisters, Mary Ann and Lorna, and a brother, Alvin, the oldest. Occasional photographs taken by her older siblings portrayed Nina's parents, Mildred and Arthur, as formal and distant from each other; Nina described them as strict and uncommunicative. Her mother looked dreary and exhausted. Her father, a traveling sales-man, was usually behind the camera. Nina described him as charming but aloof, unavailable, and rarely home.

An old adage suggests, "A picture is worth a thousand words." Nina's photos showed her looking normal and well adjusted through age nine; on her birthday that year, she was surrounded by smiling friends. By age 10, however, her head was lowered. There was no photo of her at age 11. At age 12, she was a scrawny track star. What was not visible in the photographs was that between the ages of 10 and 12 she started to starve, and then to binge and vomit. What happened in Nina's life during that time, I wondered, that no one saw?

We worked together for a year before Nina began to have memories. "Night after night he came into my room," she announced one day out of the blue.

"Night after night he came into your room," I repeated, wondering about the identity of "he," yet cautious about pressing her before she was ready to confide in me. "How old were you when this went on?"

"I don't really know." Nina's face was blank, devoid of emotion.

In this way, we began reconstructing the painful pieces of her past. Over the next few months we unearthed many facts, the first of which was that she was abused by Alvin. The sexual encounters had begun when she was 10 and he, 16.

"See yourself there, in your bed. Take a good look at your room. Take me with you."

"I see my night table with an elephant lamp on it that twirls around."

"What are you wearing?"

"I only see my head sticking out from beneath my animal quilt. Blond bunches of curly hair with red barrettes. Do you know the barrettes that little kids wear, the ones that make a snap when you close them?"

"How are you feeling?"

She paused. "Scared."

The following session, when Nina didn't appear, I checked my answering machine. She had left a message only minutes before our scheduled time. "Sorry to call so late, but I've had a terrible headache for days. I think it's the flu. See you next week." I wondered if uncovering these disturbing memories had been too distressing. Was it her body or her soul that ached? Was she avoiding me, or avoiding knowing more? I dialed her number, but there was no answer. I would have to wait until we met in person.

"That was the first appointment you've missed," I said when we next met. "How bad was your flu?"

"Just the flu," she said, describing the usual symptoms—head and body aches, exhaustion.

"I wondered if you had any more thoughts or memories about what we talked about last time."

"I must be forgetting—what did we talk about?"

"We talked about your brother, Alvin." She actually hadn't thought about him, but she did remember a nightmare.

"A nightmare?" I queried. "Any details stay with you?"

"Not really. All I can say is, I woke up with a sickening feeling about him."

"Sometimes when we *feel* sick we actually *get* sick," I said. Nina shrugged. No response. By ignoring me, she let me know how much she didn't want to deal with this. I'd have to be careful not to push her. Two months passed before she mentioned Alvin's name again.

Slowly, she became more able to recall and handle both memory and pain. In the year that followed, she recovered wisps of the past and filled in the pieces of the puzzle lost to her consciousness. She remembered:

The shaft of light, creeping into the room, expanding onto the plush carpet as the door creaked open.

A cuddly, pink nightgown with the words, "Love me, love my dog," embroidered on the pocket and her brother's hands holding her tightly beneath the soft flannel.

The shiny-covered "Dumbo" book he read to her afterwards.

As our relationship grew and she felt more secure, Nina's recollections of Alvin's nightly visits became more vivid. Sometimes she could almost feel the touch of his hands on her small breasts and the pleasurable physical sensations she experienced, which were heightened by the excitement of being wanted. These memories gnawed at her. "How could I have enjoyed even one second of it?" she asked me, her voice filled with self-disgust. I tried to help her understand that our bodies respond to certain stimuli even if our minds don't like what's happening.

Alvin's visits always began in the same ritualized manner. Late at night, after her lights were out, he would slip into her room. "Let's play hide-and-seek, Miss Special." She remembered loving his nickname for her. "How thrilling to have my handsome, brilliant brother, captain of the debating team, president of the class, all to myself!" she said one day after drifting off into a trance-like state, remembering her childhood. "How exciting to be *so* special—to be chosen by Alvin when my sisters are sleeping!"

Hide-and-seek inevitably evolved into a game of wrestling. Nina, always the winner, would sit on her brother's chest and pin him down, her knees on his shoulders. "He called me his little princess!" she remembered. His hands would free themselves and inch their way up her nightgown. First they would creep onto her knees, then up her thighs, and finally into her vagina.

Over time, he invented new twists. They reversed positions, with Nina on the floor and Alvin pinning her down. Sometimes, Alvin initiated a master-slave routine. A quick student, Nina learned to follow her brother's lead. She perfected touching him in exactly the way he needed.

"Is there more to tell?" I asked. And she responded with what was becoming a familiar shrug.

As more of the past seeped into her consciousness, Nina started to experience feelings of horror. She would look away, close her eyes, and tune out as she painstakingly described how she learned to satisfy Alvin: how to talk to, excite, and masturbate him. Bewildered by her recollections, she would ask me: *Did this happen? Really happen? Or am I imagining it?*

"Trust yourself, just be with your thoughts and feelings. Let yourself flow with them," I said, trying to reassure her.

Eventually, she remembered learning how to take her brother's penis into her mouth and spit out his semen into the purple towel he always brought into her bedroom and took with him when he left. Before leaving, he'd warn her to be silent about what had happened. "Don't you ever tell Mommy. She'll kill you for touching me!" he'd threaten, paralyzing Nina into obedience.

"Did you think your parents would have blamed you, even though you were only 10 and he was 16?" I asked, challenging one of the many distorted beliefs that contributed to her feeling of powerlessness.

"I guess so," said Nina sadly. Like so many girls who are sexually abused, she was fearful that it was her fault and she would be punished.

Two years after their midnight meetings began, Alvin left for college. Nina had already been anorexic for over a year, and a week after his departure, she collapsed, physically and emotionally depleted. She

was then taken to a physician, and shortly thereafter to her first therapist. She was in seventh grade.

I was not surprised to learn about Alvin's abuse. While many
factors can contribute to the development of an eating disorder, whenever the problem is serious and stubborn, I wonder if sexual abuse is
lurking in the past. Nina's story drove home the intricate connections
between incest and eating disorders, and as she told it, I tried to help
her understand them.

"To express outrage that your body was violated," I told her, "you
violate it yourself by depriving it of nourishment. The difference now
is that you're in charge, instead of Alvin." Nina was in control of her
anorexia, having felt out of control when she was being abused. As a
"successful" dieter, she was the master of her body, which had betrayed
her, as had her beloved brother. She was the master of her life, too,
because starving, which meant calculating what and when to eat, gave
her a focus. It kept her mind occupied and distracted from her pain. At
the same time, losing weight made her feel virtuous and accomplished,
instead of ashamed. Her anorexia was also an act of self-punishment,
for, however virtuous she felt as a dieter, like most incest victims, Nina
could not completely erase her sense of guilt. The way she saw it, even
if Alvin was the instigator, she was an accomplice in the act.

Healing involves releasing oneself from the anger and shame that
hinder growth. In addition, it involves mourning for a childhood
bereft of innocence and safety. In telling her story to me, Nina started
on the path to recovery.

Although her anorexia began when she was 10, no one in the
family paid much attention to Nina's mealtime absences or her weight
loss. When she fainted in school right before her sixth-grade graduation and the school nurse called to talk to her parents about her visible
deterioration, her mother was at first embarrassed, then furious.

"They say you've stopped eating. Is that the truth?" Mildred
demanded. Nina shrugged, and the family went on with its noisy mealtime bickering. Eventually, her sisters and, finally, Alvin himself, posed

the same question. Nina remained silent and starved—and not only for food. She was desperately hungry for more attention from her parents. She wanted them to notice her and what was happening to her.

Away at college, Alvin flourished, while Nina languished through junior and senior high school. She no longer had to suffer his nightly visits, but without him, she felt she lacked a loving connection. *Thin, thinner, thinnest,* went a song in her head, drowning out hunger, desire, and her anger at losing her position as the special sister.

Shortly after Alvin left, Nina's anorexia had transformed itself into a bulimia so unrelenting that three therapists and a hospitalization were unable to help her. "Why couldn't I have just stayed anorexic?" she asked, berating herself for being such a "disgusting failure."

"You began eating after he left because you felt so starved," I pointed out. This explanation hit home for Nina. When she realized that Alvin's touch had been nourishing as well as abusive, she also came to understand the message buried in her bulimic behavior: *Ridding herself of shameful feelings was easier than feeling them.* Her shrinking body and "shameful" habit expressed the inexpressible: "I want to be invisible; I feel disgusting." Sexual abuse victims often feel defective and dirty. They have been forced to embrace and take in another's life force. Throwing up and expelling her food may have been Nina's way of purifying herself of the poison that had been forced down her throat.

After college, Alvin attended a prestigious graduate school where he met Sally, a fellow student in his program. Shortly after completing school, they married and relocated to California. When he made his rare trips home, Nina managed to absent herself.

Upon graduating from high school, Nina enrolled in an out-of-town college. Although she had been an honor student, adjusting to university life was a nightmare. Lacking the ability to deal with her pain or to reach out to others, she floundered desperately. She returned home after only two months and enrolled in a local university, starving, isolated, and filled with a sense of failure. It was only after dropping out of another brief and disappointing experience in therapy— her third—that she contacted me at the urging of Professor Johnson.

Two years later, Nina was doing better. She was eating more regularly and her bulimic episodes were less frequent. She was seeing me twice a week as well as attending a therapy group that offered her support and membership in a healing community. Her journal had become a sanctuary in which she explored her past:

> *I felt so isolated. I couldn't eat and didn't know why. I began skipping dinner, then breakfast. I prayed someone would ask me why I wasn't eating, but no one did. What's hindered my recovery the most is being so skilled at being silent. The tragedy is, first he silenced me, and then I silenced myself.*

Then, on her 23rd birthday, she received the news that Alvin's marriage was over, and he was coming home. Nina's mother was overjoyed. "How lucky we are to have Al home again," she crooned. Nina promptly lost two pounds.

"How are you feeling about his return?" I asked Nina repeatedly, but to my dismay, the only answer I got was that she was fine.

Alvin arrived and uttered barely a word about his failed marriage and bitter divorce. Soon after, Mildred and Arthur left for a long-planned African safari, leaving Nina alone with her brother. The day before they left, she stopped eating altogether. By the time they returned, she was one pound away from another hospitalization.

"What are you saying with your body that you need to put into words?" I asked at our next session, but my question fell on deaf ears. Nina had no answer. However much she knew by now about her disorder, and however much insight she had gained into herself, she still knew no better way of coping than to translate her unacceptable feelings into a bitter-tasting but tolerable hatred of fat. Clearly, her issues with the incest were still dangerously alive. I racked my brain for a way to help her.

For a long time, I had been hoping that Nina would consider revealing the incest to her parents. I was encouraged by the fact that, although initially she spoke of it only with me, over time her "comfort zone" had expanded. First, she confided in the therapy group members.

Later, she wrote a paper about incest and eating disorders in a psychology course she was taking.

Doing the research helped her understand herself better. After reading the paper to the group and me, she felt more comfortable revealing her sense of betrayal, anger, and sorrow to others. Her next audience was her boyfriend, whose outraged and angry response helped to validate her own feelings. Then, she read the paper to her medical doctor. Finally, after Alvin's return home and Nina's relapse, a member of our therapy group suggested that she talk with her parents.

Nina was reluctant. Alvin had always been her mother's favorite. Why would her parents believe her? What if he denied abusing her? Nevertheless, supported by the group, her boyfriend, and me, she gathered up her courage once again. She knew that to free herself from her eating disorder she needed to be able to speak honestly and openly about her feelings, rather than use her body to communicate them.

Timidly, she invited her parents to come in for a family session and, reluctantly, they agreed. Although Nina and I spent a great deal of time talking and planning for the big moment, we were completely unprepared for what would occur.

Some sessions leave a lasting impression; this was one. After we all settled in, Nina introduced the session with a confident, powerful opening. "I know you never really understood my eating disorder," she said, looking straight into her parents' eyes, "and that's not entirely your fault. I have kept some of the facts from you—facts that have helped me understand myself and, I hope, will help you understand me, too." A long pause followed. "When I was little," she continued, "Alvin abused me."

Slowly, without faltering, she spelled out the details, but a stony silence greeted her revelation. She stopped speaking with tears trickling down her face. I had anticipated that she might have difficulty staying grounded and focused, and as planned, I jumped in to explain the link between Nina's sexual abuse and her bingeing and purging. I began with the bingeing.

"When Nina was abused by Alvin, whom she loved, she learned to distrust love," I said. "Betrayed by a loved one, she was afraid to turn to others for love. So, instead, she turned to food. When she binges, she is seeking love."

Next, I addressed the purging. "Being sexually abused taught Nina another harsh lesson: Her body was a betrayer. When she purges, she punishes her body." I then explained how Nina's starving served many functions. "When she starves, she denies her need for love and support and she remembers she is alone. This mirrors how she felt when she was abused: alone and without support."

While I spoke, Nina regained her strength. She said that being silent continued to harm her, perhaps as much as the abuse itself. Her silence kept her isolated and ashamed. It also left her vulnerable to being abused by others. Her shame remained deeply intertwined with her self-punishing behavior. It was crucial, she told them, that she tell them the truth now. But her parents were deadened to her.

"He wouldn't, couldn't have done that! Not our Alvin!" her mother cried in disbelief.

"You must have imagined it. Perhaps you wanted it!" her father accused.

"Not our Alvin!" insisted her mother again.

Finally, her father turned to me with a contemptuous challenge that signaled the end of our session. "I don't like to contest you, Doctor, but if it wasn't penetration, it doesn't sound like sexual abuse to me."

Her parents' icy stares will be forever etched in my mind. Neither of them spoke for several moments, and in that uncomfortable space, I recalled the words of a wise supervisor who emphasized two principles that have stayed with me: The cruelest loss of all is the loss of hope; and the opposite of love is not hatred, but indifference. In that moment, as I sat with Nina and her parents, I gained a new respect for the devastating power of both.

Nina's head sank lower and lower. Denial and disgust had greeted her revelation. Mildred and Arthur had sent us a clear message: There would be no further discussions. In a businesslike manner, they stood, shook my hand, and left. The issue was closed. Nina, her sexual abuse, and I were dismissed.

Afterwards, Nina and I sat in silence. A sense of defeat filled the room. I guessed that she was hurt and angry with her parents—and perhaps with me, too. "Now do you see?" she asked tearfully. I did.

Nina had come alone to this family session, and alone she left on this rainy, cold November night. Drained, I sat in my chair. The room was empty, but the haunted look in her eyes as we said goodbye lingered in my mind. Had I done her more harm than good by encouraging her to arrange this meeting?

I was overcome with worry. If the session had hit *me* with such force, what was Nina feeling? How would she handle her parents' outright rejection of her truth, one that had taken her years to uncover and months to become strong enough to share with them? Would she be able to tolerate her despair and disappointment?

Wearily, I closed my eyes, but not to rest. "Your judgment was off," I heard my inner voice chiding me as I reviewed the session. I had always believed that healing is rooted in truth-telling, because relationships can suffer when there are secrets. But my efforts to heal the rift between Nina and her parents had backfired. While Mildred and Arthur firmly and brutally disavowed what had happened to their daughter, I was helpless to affect the unfolding family drama.

Perhaps I had become just one more person who let Nina down. On the other hand, maybe seeing me stand up to her parents as her advocate would help her value our connection to each other and empower her to do the same. Seeing me survive failure in the face of her parents' unshakable version of reality might allow her to risk failing, too. And knowing that they treated me just the same way that they treated her could help her see that the problem wasn't her, it was them. With little closure or consolation, I finally forced myself to leave both my office and these troubling thoughts.

The next morning, my first call was from Nina. "He knows," she blurted into the phone.

"*Who* knows?" I asked.

Nobody could have been more surprised than I was by the story that she told me. The previous night, deeply distressed after our session, she had come home and sought refuge writing on the computer, which she had recently started to use for her journal entries. Afterwards, she printed out the sexual abuse paper she had written for psychology class. When Alvin came home later that night, he went to use the computer and found the paper. After he had finished reading, he knocked on Nina's door. In tears, he expressed remorse and begged for forgiveness. Nina was stunned.

"I've never seen him so upset. He said he'd do anything to help— even go to therapy with me!"

A rich series of events ensued. Upset, but eager to help, Alvin joined Nina for several sessions in my office, where he expressed his regret and shame, and offered profuse apologies. Most important, he corroborated Nina's account of what had happened, the story that she herself had sometimes found hard to believe. At first, Nina was quick to forgive him, but I encouraged her to slow down, get in touch with her feelings of rage, shame, and grief, and share them with him. I wanted her forgiveness to be genuine, and we can only truly forgive after we've communicated our anger. By directly expressing all her feelings, perhaps she could release herself from the need to reenact the trauma she had suffered.

Healing is a process, not an event. Remembering facts, releasing pent-up feelings of rage and hurt, and integrating those feelings into our being is a long, tedious process that occurs in unpredictable waves. Sometimes it moves along quickly; at other times, it drags. At first, Nina was passive and only tentatively expressed her shame. After a few sessions, though, she grew stronger and started to talk about the ripples caused by what Alvin had done to her beginning when she was 10 years old. She described how the abuse had left her with a lack of trust that continued to permeate her relationships, especially with her current boyfriend. Being violated made her feel worthless; she still felt that way at times. In response, she deprived herself of food as well as a host of nourishing and pleasurable experiences. She seldom enjoyed sex. She hated her body. She couldn't stop depriving and hurting herself.

As Nina spoke, I encouraged her to direct her words not to me, but to Alvin, who sat next to her on the couch, looking deeply pained. "Explain how feeling out of control affected you," I'd suggest softly, "and how you are still scared of so many things." By confronting him and seeing the look of anguish on his face, she came to own her story in a new way.

The focus of our sessions gradually shifted to Alvin, for, in listening to Nina, he became more reflective. First, he listened to her with understanding and remorse. Her openness caused him to reach out, sometimes comforting her, at other times expressing his own feelings of humiliation and regret. I encouraged him to talk, and soon he poured out the details of his failed marriage. Then, a portrait of a frightened young boy emerged, socially awkward and shy. At 16, Alvin had been curious about girls, yet incredibly insecure.

"I was all sizzle, no steak," he said sadly. Although he was the valedictorian and star athlete of his high-school class, he had had no real friends. "Perhaps I turned to you out of desperation," he told Nina. "I really didn't know that what I was doing was wrong."

"How could you not have known it was wrong?" she demanded. He couldn't answer, only ask for her acceptance. He really didn't know. Through his apology and attention to her suffering, he finally helped Nina realize that she was not responsible for what had happened. She didn't have to punish herself.

One day, Nina and Alvin came in with the same photo album that she had used to introduce me to her family. Sitting side by side with the album on Nina's knobby knees, she and her brother examined the evidence and unearthed the roots of their unhappy childhood. They shared memories of being ignored by busy, self-absorbed parents who consistently pressured them to achieve and cause no trouble. They also realized the extent to which they had been driven to seek comfort from each other in ways that were ultimately damaging. Together, they mourned. Once again, I was amazed by the infinite ways that healing can occur.

Nina came to therapy with a short story about a sad girl and her mother, and left with a story about the girl and her sad brother. The first story remained unresolved; therapy doesn't change everything, but through it, Nina learned to look elsewhere than to her parents for understanding and support. She found it in an unexpected place. I never would have guessed that the brother who had abused her would end up offering her the validation that she needed. Perhaps, a part of her always had harbored the hope that healing was possible. I'll always wonder if that hope took charge the night after the shattering session with her parents and *arranged* for Alvin to find the computer printout that spelled out her problems. I like to think so, because it would mean that, after two years of therapy, she was ready to risk writing a new chapter in her life in which she took control without starving or purging. Sitting in my office across from Nina and Alvin, and looking at her skinny legs which balanced the weighty family album, I saw in her the germ of a new identity, one based not on being invisible, but on being honored and respected for speaking her truth.

2

A Crack
in the Wall

The sorrow that has no vent in
tears makes other organs weep.
—HENRY MAUDSLEY

Growing up is a precarious journey. Especially during the teenage years, children hit occasional rocky patches as they struggle to come to grips with their changing bodies and fast-paced lives. Many young people's inner resources are stretched to the limit by all that they have to deal with, but if they can draw strength from the people closest to them, especially their parents, they usually manage to ride the ups and downs. However, some cannot make nourishing connections with anyone, least of all their parents, because they have built a protective wall around themselves. Chipping down that wall is a long, painstaking process . . .

"It's Marilyn Schwartz again. I hate to bother you with so many messages, but I have to talk to you about my daughter. It's urgent. Please call."

Replaying my answering machine on that cold November night, I listened to the three messages from the same unfamiliar caller. She sounded desperate. Even more than her words, her tone of voice drummed on my heart.

Dialing her number, I glanced at the time—just after 11 P.M. *Should I be calling a new patient at this hour?* Would she think I was a workaholic or just disorganized? "Over-extended" was closer to the truth. With two children to carpool, errands to run, dinner to fix, and homework to supervise, in addition to seeing clients, returning calls sometimes got lost in the blur.

When I introduced myself, Mrs. Schwartz sounded relieved. "Thank you for getting back to me at this late hour," she said. "I'm truly grateful." A muffled sob punctuated a long silence. "Forgive me for breaking down. It's my daughter, Mia. She's 19, and we're in trouble." Mia and her mother had been seeing a psychiatrist, Dr. Laufer, for six months. "I don't think he understands her, me, or anything at all about her problem—bulimia."

Just that day Marilyn had telephoned Dr. Laufer about a snag in the insurance reimbursement. The call was an eye-opener because she discovered that he hadn't seen Mia in two weeks. "When I confronted her, Mia said she stopped going because she wasn't getting anything out of it. Then she stormed out of the room, sneering, 'You can't make me go back.' Of course, she's right. I can't make her."

"You certainly can't," I agreed.

"She dropped out of college last May, right before finals. As soon as she came home, all she could talk about was how fat she was, even though she was painfully thin. I didn't pay a lot of attention to her and her 'fat' talk, but now I realize I should have. I work in a high school and know about eating disorders, but when it came to my own daughter, I was in the dark. I think she might even be taking laxatives. That's a symptom of bulimia, right?"

Before I could respond, she continued breathlessly. "Mia hasn't had her period in six months. She's 5'7" and weighs only 107 pounds, so I'm worried. She's impossible to get along with, too. She's always moody and can be really nasty. Another thing—she just lost her job, the third since she dropped out of school. And the bathrooms . . ."

"Let's stop right here," I interrupted, feeling overwhelmed. "You've got a lot going on. Why don't we set up an appointment?"

"That's part of the problem," said Mrs. Schwartz. "She's had it with shrinks."

"Does she know you're calling me?" I asked. Mia did not. "Without knowing you or Mia, it's difficult to give you advice," I told her, wondering whether Marilyn was afraid to push her daughter too hard and risk making her angry. Perhaps she was worried that she would lose her. "As a start, try being open and honest. Tell her in a straightforward way exactly what you see—she's lost weight, is hardly eating, and seems unhappy. Let her know you're worried."

Mrs. Schwartz's frustration spilled over. "I just told you—she won't listen to anyone, especially me! She thinks I'm a loser."

"Raising kids is *not* easy," I said. "Let me make a suggestion. Tell her you called me because you love her and are concerned about her. Take care not to let her think therapy is a punishment for bad behavior—let her know it's more of a gift. If she still won't see me, why don't you come in first and we'll see if we can get her to follow? How does that sound?"

Marilyn paused. "If it's *her* problem, why would *I* come in?"

"Because you're her mother and you are worried that she's in danger. When Mia hurts, so do you. You're right, it is her problem, but she's not ready to do anything, and you are. So let's give it a try. Are you available Thursday at 5:30?"

Marilyn Schwartz introduced herself with a firm handshake and a wide smile, but as she sat down and began speaking, her voice shook.

"Obviously, Mia refused to come in," she told me. "I couldn't get her to budge and I'm at my wit's end."

"How do you usually get her to do things you want her to do, like chores around the house?" I asked. Although bulimia is clearly a more serious problem than a messy room, I wanted Marilyn to see that her everyday parenting skills might help get Mia into therapy. But my question bombed. Marilyn no longer considered herself an effective parent in any arena.

"You've got to be kidding. She doesn't listen to anyone, especially me. That's why I'm here! Her bulimia is getting worse, no doubt about that. There's something else, too. Yesterday I found some matchbooks in her car. I wouldn't have thought twice about it, but I saw another pack on her bureau, and she doesn't even smoke. I asked myself, *Why matches?* Then I remembered a newspaper article about kids cutting and burning themselves on purpose. It seems that's the new 'rage.' I asked Mia if she was burning herself, and she denied it, but I don't know whether to believe her."

Marilyn sounded frantic and I was growing increasingly concerned. Although I had never treated anyone who had self-mutilated, I did know it could be a serious problem. But before I could respond, Marilyn had moved on to her next complaint.

"She's out until all hours of the night with her boyfriend, Brett. When she's home, she's usually in her room, which is a mess, eating or sleeping. I can't count on her for anything. If I ask her to do any chores while I'm at work, forget it. Often she doesn't get out of bed until I get home." Marilyn's voice sounded like the moan of a wounded animal.

"And when you two do get together?"

"I never know what to expect. If I knock on her door, she'll either scream at me to go away or be happy to see me." One recent evening, Marilyn had come home to find Mia crying hysterically. "She was standing there in front of the mirror, staring at herself, grabbing her thighs as if they were pieces of meat, and shrieking, 'How am I going to get rid of this flab?' She can spend hours berating herself for what she calls her 'fat.'"

"How do you handle this?" I asked.

"Sometimes I tell her, 'Mia, everyone has parts of their body they dislike—we just learn to live with them!' Or I'll say, 'Listen, Mia, I hate parts of my body, too. Take a look at the flab under my arms and my sagging chin.' I tell her that other people don't even notice the parts of our bodies that bother us. Is that wrong for me to say?"

Although Marilyn's dissatisfaction with her own body wasn't unusual, it was making me increasingly uncomfortable. Research has consistently concluded that mothers who are self-critical of their own bodies send unspoken messages to their daughters that their bodies, too, are not good enough. Eventually, Marilyn would need to help her daughter feel proud of herself for who she was on the inside, and she could start by not focusing on Mia's appearance. For example, when Mia complained about her weight, Marilyn could change the subject and ask about her interests or friends. But this was not the time to give Marilyn a lesson on parenting.

"You sound really worried about Mia," I said. "Why don't you tell me what's been going on?"

Six months earlier, Mia had dropped out of college and come home announcing she was a vegetarian. Marilyn had joined her. "It may sound weird to you," Marilyn told me, "but I saw it as a way we could do something positive together, maybe become better friends. Besides, I'm always a fan of anything that can help me lose weight, but like everything else, it became a catastrophe. Everything I did was wrong— how I cooked, how I arranged the refrigerator. I used the wrong oil in the salad dressing, the cheese I bought wasn't low-fat enough. We had arguments galore. How could I have known a simple diet would become such a disaster?"

"You sound like you're blaming yourself," I noted, "and that's not going to help her or you." I assured her that many parents don't notice when a child's normal eating slides into disordered eating. It can happen so subtly that even professionals have a hard time picking it up.

"In developing an eating disorder," I explained, "your daughter is telling you that something is wrong, but she doesn't know what it is. It looks like food is the problem, but in reality, an eating disorder is about unbearable feelings. In coming back home to live, she's telling you that she isn't ready to be out on her own and she needs you. Her eating disorder is speaking for her, and she's lucky, because you are hearing her. She's giving you a second chance to help her grow up."

Perhaps my words offered Marilyn the comfort and safety she needed to open up further. "I haven't even begun to tell you what it's really like for *me*. It's not just the messy bathrooms and the empty refrigerator. She has crazy screaming matches with her boyfriend. Whenever he's over they fight like maniacs. I'm living in a loony bin."

I was delighted. Now Marilyn was focusing on how Mia's problems impacted *her*. I wanted her to realize that she had choices and was *letting* her daughter make her life miserable. In fact, she was allowing Mia to treat her the way Mia treated herself—with disrespect.

"How long has it been like a loony bin?" I asked.

"A very long time," she said, struggling to contain her tears. "I hate sounding like a victim, because I'm not really that type." But as her story unfolded, it was clear that she was a survivor and had good reason to feel victimized. She had suddenly found herself a widow when her 34-year-old husband, Charlie, suffered a fatal heart attack. "It happened the Saturday after Thanksgiving, just 16 years ago." The painstaking detail with which she described finding her husband gasping for breath on the kitchen floor alerted me to the fact that after all these years, the horror of Charlie's death was still raw. At 32, Marilyn was left with three small children to raise, Mia being the youngest. The funeral, in fact, had been on Mia's first day of kindergarten.

Marilyn was biting her lip. "There's more," she went on. "The month after Charlie died, my mother was diagnosed with terminal cancer." Her face looked frozen. When I asked her how she had coped, she replied, "I don't want to talk about it." I felt as if an impenetrable wall had suddenly gone up—a wall she must have built years ago to protect her from unbearable grief.

Single-parenting three children, in addition to teaching full-time, had been an overwhelming load, more than Marilyn had bargained for. She had previously relied on Charlie for setting rules, and could muster little energy of her own to rule the roost. Her solution to exhaustion was to be easy-going. "I was never a great disciplinarian, but together, we were a great team," she said. "Maybe I gave them too much freedom." <u>Listening to her, I thought about the fine line separating freedom from neglect</u>.

In contrast to her two older brothers, both of whom were born with Attention Deficit and Hyperactivity Disorder, Mia had been the easiest of three—until now. When she was a child, her mother had nicknamed her "The Unsqueaky Wheel." "She was always my little helper," Marilyn told me. I suspected the Unsqueaky Wheel hadn't gotten enough oil. Being undemanding in a hectic home, she was easily overlooked, and growing up without basic emotional nourishment—time and attention—left her unprepared for the challenges of going away to college and living independently. The eating disorder offered her a way to get from her mother what she so desperately wanted, but couldn't ask for—the day-to-day attention and concern that children translate into a sense of security and love.

"You've had to deal with a lot," I said, "between the boys' hyperactivity, Charlie's death, your mother's illness and death, and the financial responsibility for your family. You have a lot of strength, and I'm sure you are going to get through this, too." I hoped my voice conveyed that I was in awe of her ability to cope.

I suggested that she ask Mia again whether she had ever burned herself. People usually burn and cut themselves for the same reasons they binge on food, starve themselves, drink, or do drugs, I explained—they can't manage their angry, sad, lonely feelings. "Keep your eyes open for any burn mark or cuts. If she acts as if you're being nosy, don't back off. Keep asking questions. It will let Mia know you care and are concerned."

Considering Mia's attitude, another attempt at family therapy seemed premature. Instead, I encouraged Marilyn to attend a group for parents of eating-disordered youngsters. "Meeting with other parents will give you the support I think *you* need." Marilyn's eyes flickered with what I thought was a glimmer of hope. She impressed me as a woman with both common sense and the capacity to care. I kept my fingers crossed.

Three weeks later Marilyn returned, again without her daughter, but she seemed in better spirits. She had been reading one of the books I'd recommended and was bubbling with ideas. *Surviving an Eating Disorder: New Perspectives and Strategies for Family and Friends* was helping her insist that Mia become more involved in and responsible for household chores. Marilyn had also attended two sessions of the parent group, which helped her realize that being a "softy" didn't help Mia. "Some of those people are really tough!" she said. "They don't take being pushed around by their kids at all."

When Marilyn had discussed the "loony bin" with the group, they'd given her some pretty strong advice. For example, one parent described how she held her daughter responsible for cleaning the bathroom after she vomited. Another suggested that Marilyn insist Mia replace any food she used up during a binge. These rules might seem trivial in the light of a serious problem like bulimia, but I have often seen a young-ster make dramatic progress with her eating disorder when a parent alters his or her overall approach. Sometimes enforcing a simple rule about cleaning up the bathroom or replacing food creates a ripple effect. If Marilyn could begin demanding that Mia respect her, per-haps Mia would eventually learn to respect herself.

Before she left, I showed Marilyn a plaque in my office that a pa-tient had given me, inscribed with the words, *There are only two gifts a parent gives her child: roots and wings*.

"Expecting more from your daughter will help Mia develop the roots she needs in order to fly. You need to find a way to do something special with her that doesn't involve food or losing weight—and don't forget to ask her about the burning." Marilyn nodded in agreement. If we were lucky, Mia would realize that decisions affecting her life were being made in this office, and she'd consider coming in.

One month later, Mia called.

My stomach dropped as I greeted the tall, skinny girl with stringy hair, dirty fingernails, and multiple piercings in both ears and her left eyebrow. She wore filthy, ripped dungarees and a t-shirt that proclaimed in bold letters, "If you hate loud music, you must be old." I had met plenty of teenagers who made dramatic statements with their bodies, but Mia's seemed unusually harsh. She clearly broadcast the message, "Don't even think about being nice to me because I'm not very nice."

After we sat down in my office, she announced in a belligerent tone, "I'm just here for my mom. She thinks I need help. I told her that I'd go this one time just to shut her up. Personally, I don't think anything could make a difference. This is just one big waste of time."

"If you think this is a waste of time, I certainly understand why you wouldn't want to come back." I said. After a short pause I added, "You probably have some good reasons for thinking this won't work."

"That's exactly right," she said defiantly. "That other doctor. He didn't tell me anything I don't know. And he was a loser—all wrong about my personality. He didn't understand anything about me."

"What didn't he understand?" I asked.

"Everything," she shot back. "I'm really shy. I might not seem shy right now, but I am. I have no goals. And that doctor didn't understand that I don't *need* goals and I have no desire to 'apply myself,' as he called it! He bugged me. 'You're damaging your body!' he'd say. Then he'd lecture me about my teeth—warn me they'd rot right out of my head! What a waste of 45 minutes. I'd shut him out."

"How did you do that?" I wondered.

"I'd put up a wall—that's easy for me." *Just like her mother,* I thought, recalling how Marilyn had coped with life after her husband's death.

"How?"

"I can look like I'm here, but I'm not," she said. I thought she suppressed a smile.

"You're tough," I said, "but I think I just saw a crack in the wall." This time her smile was clearly visible. Even though Mia was perfectly aware of the fact that she built walls around herself, what she didn't know was that they separated her from her true emotions, as did her bingeing and vomiting. I hoped our relationship would give her an opportunity to understand what she was doing; drawing attention to the times that she created walls between herself and me was a first step. Eventually, we might even learn how she could break through her walled-off stance.

"Did you ever let Doctor Laufer see behind your wall?"

"That idiot? No way!"

"You really sound angry!" I wanted to let her know that I accepted and welcomed her anger. I wasn't afraid of it the way her mother was, nor was I about to lecture her.

"That's right, I'm angry," she said, her pitch mounting. "He was too old and too backwards and too off-base."

"Off-base?"

"That's right! He'd say, 'You're living on the edge just to be different!' He thought I was competing with my mother and that I'm angry 'cause I can never be like her." As she vented her feelings about being misunderstood, first by her mother, then by Dr. Laufer, I felt as if a dam had burst.

"You know the movie, *The Best Little Girl in the World*? Well, I became the worst little girl in the world. I started out like a precious doll. By the time I was in high school, I became a brat and wound up a real juvenile delinquent—drinking, smoking, cutting school, and hanging out in bars. My mother couldn't do anything about it."

"It sounds like a lonely kind of fun," I said. She nodded. I remembered her mother's description of the young Mia as especially easy to handle. Sometimes children who feel that they have to be the good, responsible ones, when everything around them is chaos, miss out on normal childhood rebelliousness, until later. "Is there anyone who understands you?" She shook her head, no. "What about your boyfriend?" I asked.

"Brett? He's a pain in my butt and he *never* listens to me." How often had I heard a bulimic patient complain that someone in their life "wasn't listening," when in reality the patient had not revealed her true feelings?

Mia was now on a roll. She talked about her bulimia with a surprising candor. "I started vomiting as soon as I went away to school. I heard about bingeing and purging in high school, but it had always grossed me out. I don't know why, but I started doing it. When I got to college, half of the girls on my floor were throwing up. Some were burning themselves, too."

My ears perked up. I took a risk and asked, "Did you ever try burning yourself?" She shook her head and went back to talking about the bulimia, leaving me to wonder.

Kids come into contact with all kinds of addictions and self-abusive practices during their first years of college. Food, drugs, alcohol—some kids try one, others try them all as a way of dealing with the fact that they feel lost and overwhelmed by their new experiences, or are desperately homesick. What can begin as a seemingly innocent experiment with cutting and burning can quickly spin into serious self-mutilation. Now that Mia had mentioned burning, I was frightened. Many people are terribly ashamed of the fact that they hurt themselves, and the shame prevents them from acknowledging their behavior, even to themselves. Although Mia had denied burning, as I had advised Marilyn, I might have to raise this question again.

Between the first and second sessions, Mia had told her girlfriend Brenda about me, but not about her bulimia. "Brenda goes to OA—she's at least 100 pounds overweight," were her opening words. "She really could use you!"

"That sounds almost like a compliment," I said.

"Well, you're better than that other guy," she admitted, and then she was off again, heaping abuse on Doctor Laufer. As I listened, I heard the same anger behind her words: He didn't understand me, my mom doesn't understand me, and no one ever will.

"That's *just* how I feel," she told me sadly.

"And you came back anyway," I said. No reply.

"You know," I went on, "after you left last time, I was concerned. You mentioned burning, and when I met with your mom, she was concerned about that, too. Did she mention anything to you?" Mia paused, and I held my breath, hoping she wouldn't feel betrayed by her mother.

"There's not much to say." I thought I detected a flicker of sadness, but by the time she spoke again, it was gone. "Yeah, I burned myself a few times when I was away at school. No big deal. No big deal at all," she said with a glibness that I didn't quite trust.

"Tell me about no big deal."

Mia shrugged and moved back to her bulimia. "I hate being bulimic and I hate admitting that I hate it, too."

"Wait a minute," I interrupted. "The burning—no big deal?"

"Exactly," she said firmly. "And besides, I'm over that. It's the bulimia that gets to me. I want to stop, but I can't, and no one understands, especially my mother. She thinks I could stop if I really tried."

I felt suspended between my agenda, the burning, and hers, the bulimia. Fortunately, a little voice whispered, *Listen to her! Don't be pushy and make the mistake that Dr. Laufer made or she won't come back.*

"Sorry," I said. "I think I was just off-base." Mia smiled, and I felt I had regained our connection. "About your bulimia. Your mother thinks you can just stop . . . but I'm not so sure. If you *could* stop, you wouldn't be here, right?" She nodded. "But when you're ready to stop, you will. Perhaps you're not quite ready yet?"

That puzzled her. "I want to stop but I can't, and that scares me. The other night I saw *The Karen Carpenter Story* on TV. She wanted to stop and she died, right?" I nodded. More details poured out: vomiting, laxatives, cramps, diarrhea, secrecy, and pain. "It's serious, right?"

"Bulimia is serious," I said, "and you've already handled a serious problem—losing your dad."

She laughed. "You know what my way of handling problems is—I put up my wall. At home, I close my mother out. Or I run away. That's what I did up at school. I ran away when I thought I would flunk out. I quit my last job because I hate getting up in the morning. I can't get up because I'm so tired from throwing up. I even run away from my friends; I've stopped going out to dinner with them because I can't handle vomiting in public bathrooms."

"So how long have you had this wall?" I asked her.

"I don't know," she said, "but I never worry about important things. All I worry about is what to eat and when I'll get down to 100 pounds, even though I know it's ridiculous to want to weigh so little and be 5'7". I don't really know why, but I keep on throwing up."

"You sound like you know more about this than you think you do. I wonder what we'd be talking about if we weren't talking about your bulimia?"

She shrugged. "Who knows?"

After a few moments of silence, I said, "That's something for us to consider—what these other problems might be. We can let them sit on the back burner for now. The first issue is your tendency to run away." I intended to be as firm with Mia as I had asked Marilyn to be and provide Mia with a consistent message: *We care, and we don't want you to slip through the cracks.* "Running away is not going to work here, not if you really want to get better."

Mia assured me that she did, indeed, want to get better and agreed to come in for weekly therapy sessions. Incredibly, before leaving, she also agreed to make appointments with a medical doctor and a registered dietitian.

"Everyone has bad habits," I told Mia. "The good news is that habits can be changed. Did you ever bite your nails?" She had. "Me, too," I said. "If you bite your nails, you can stop. If you smoke, you can stop. If you have bulimia, you can get over it—if you're willing to do hard work." Mia assured me that she *was* willing and that she had no intention of dropping out of therapy. This was good news. At the same time, though, I didn't think that she was ready to hear about the other piece of the puzzle: Bad habits generally cover wounds.

"Let's look at the job situation," I said when Mia returned the following week. "Not working and being at home sleeping all day keeps you barricaded from the world. It doesn't sound like a good way for you to spend your time or recover." I held my breath and was pleasantly surprised when she smiled at me.

Although bulimia reflects deeper issues, sometimes it's better to wait for a later phase of therapy before attempting to understand them. For now, as long she was staying home with nothing to do but eat and throw up, she was not going to get better no matter how much we talked about her feelings. Perhaps getting a job would also help her feel less like a "loser."

"What do you like to do?" I asked.

"Nothing," she said.

I asked her to tell me about all the jobs she had ever held.

"All I can do is waitress, which I don't want to do." Mia had quit three waitressing jobs within the past few months. She'd been working at the last restaurant only a few days when she walked out because a supervisor spoke to her harshly. She wasn't sorry. "Those jobs were totally wrong for me. Imagine the temptation, being around food all day."

"You make quick decisions," I said, wanting to gently point out her tendency to be impulsive.

"That's what my mom always says—'Mia never thinks before she acts.'"

"I didn't say that, exactly, but I think you can find a job that doesn't tempt you," I encouraged her. "You'll just have to get out from behind that wall you're hiding behind." She grinned. "Tell me more about which jobs you've liked and which ones you've hated."

Eventually, Mia recalled working as an assistant to the swimming counselor at a day camp when she was 16. "There was a little girl there I think I really helped." Six-year-old Jessica had developed a fear of the pool after her grandmother died, and refused to go swimming. While the other kids were splashing in the water, Mia baby-sat her and they would talk.

"What did you make of her fear?" I asked.

Mia told me that Jessica had been very close to her grandmother, who was like a second mother to her. "I thought maybe she was heart-broken," Mia said.

"That's a powerful word, heartbroken," I commented. "I'm thinking about you—you had a grandmother who died when you were young, too."

"I don't remember her," said Mia.

"Kids can get really messed up when they are young and lose their grandparents . . . or their parents," I added. She nodded. "You lost your father when you were even younger than Jessica."

"It's funny that you bring that up," she said. "I was just thinking about him, too."

"What were you thinking?" I asked, but she shrugged me off.

"I think you just went behind your wall."

"I don't want to talk about it," she said, and I heard the echo of her mother's voice.

Two months and many newspaper ads later, Mia found a position in a day-care center as an assistant teacher. Although the hours were long, the pay low, and the work physically tiring and emotionally draining, she was pleased with herself. A different-looking Mia emerged: clean hair, clean clothes, softer.

After she had been at her job for a few weeks, she told me that she was beginning to feel more comfortable around food. By now she was seeing a nutritionist regularly, and her bulimic episodes were slowly and steadily diminishing. Keeping set hours helped her develop new routines around eating, she said, and working eight hours a day didn't leave much time for vomiting. Also, she and her mother were fighting less. All of this helped her to feel more in control of her life.

Unfortunately, though, when a patient is making progress with one problem, others often emerge. After all, people develop self-abusive behaviors for a reason: They help them to cope.

Mia arrived 25 minutes late for our next session.

"I have to tell you something," she said. "But I can't."

"Try," I encouraged her, and slowly she rolled up one sleeve to uncover a small, round Band-Aid. "I did it Sunday night with a cigarette," she whispered.

"It must have hurt like hell," I said, wincing as an image of her seared skin flashed into my mind.

Mia shrugged. She couldn't remember if it hurt. I felt ill. How sad that she had put herself through all this physical pain to numb her emotional pain. Of course, it hadn't made her feel any better.

"Tell me how you felt when you were burning yourself," I suggested. I deliberately didn't ask Mia to describe *how* she had burned herself, because I was afraid that focusing on the graphic details would glorify the behavior and divert her attention from the underlying issues. I *did* want her to start putting her emotional hurts into language, though. The more she could discover the messages she was sending, the more likely she would gain a true sense of control and mastery by facing her needs and feelings in a direct way.

She told me that Brett had stormed out of her house Friday night and hadn't called all weekend. "Try to remember exactly how you felt when you did it," I repeated, because connecting the feelings with the behavior was the hard part.

"I don't remember."

Mia had stayed home Saturday and slept. On Sunday she went to the mall with her friends. "When I got home, I flipped on the TV and there was a girl about to slit her wrist because her boyfriend had left her. I saw some matches lying on the table and I remembered when I burned myself before. The idea just came into my mind. As crazy as it sounds, I felt relaxed after I did it. Do you think I'm crazy?"

"I think you're scared."

I was pleased that Mia felt comfortable enough with me to share her secret, but I was scared, too. We had come so far, but now we had a new crisis on our hands.

Mia's ability to describe this painful story without a trace of feeling did not surprise me; after all, she was an expert at disconnecting from her internal hurts. The wounds on her arm, like her bulimia, were visible proof of her success in walling herself off from her body, as well as her emotions. While she was burning or vomiting, she was in a dissociated state. Neither her physical nor emotional pain existed.

There are different kinds of self-injurers. Some, like Mia, do not register the physical or emotional pain. Others are distracted from their emotional pain by the pain of the body. The act of self-injury itself can either be "planned" or spontaneous. In all cases, though, the behavior is a survival tool that helps individuals cope when their lives feel oppressive. Self-injurers say that their behaviors "show" how much pain they are suffering in a way that language cannot.

"Let's look at the relationship between Brett and burning yourself," I suggested, when Mia returned the next day for an additional session. "What did you do after he left?" I wasn't surprised to learn that she went into her room and "tried" to listen to a new Grateful Dead CD. She explained that she couldn't remember much because her mind had gone blank.

"Like throwing up, burning is a way of not talking about, or even thinking about, how you feel. They're both your way of expressing, through your body, what's going on inside," I said, wanting Mia to see this connection. Over half of all self-injurers are bulimic, and in both cases, one goal of therapy is to expose the emotional hurt that the physical hurt is masking.

"How about we look at what you were feeling when he left?" No response. "What do you think you were feeling before you burned yourself?" Mia shrugged and looked away. "Just take a minute and think about what it was like, coming home from the mall. What were you thinking and feeling when you walked in the door?"

Mia finally burst out tearfully. "I was missing Brett. I missed him the whole day and I kept calling my machine, but he hadn't left me any messages." Later she learned that he, too, had been miserable and out drinking all weekend with his friends.

"So what do you think you would have been feeling if you *hadn't* burned yourself?" I asked. Mia began to cry.

I was relieved to learn that Mia's burning behavior hadn't been going on for a long time. In fact, she said she had only burned herself on two previous occasions. The first time had been a year earlier, during the fall Homecoming Weekend. I hoped that she was telling me the truth. While self-mutilation is serious, sufferers can get better, especially if the problem is not chronic. Most important is dealing with the problem rather than hiding it. Nevertheless, I wondered about the matches that her mother had mentioned. Had Mia been playing with the idea of burning herself as a way of distracting herself when troublesome issues arose?

"Brett couldn't come up for Homecoming, so I accepted a date with another guy, Jeb, who called at the last minute and said he was sick. Of course, I didn't believe him for a second. He just changed his mind. The whole dorm was empty and I was alone. Brett hadn't called me in three days and I felt horrible. I was sitting in my room smoking a cigarette and trying to figure out what to do, and the next thing, I was burning my arm." She had been careful to burn only her upper arm so that she could hide the marks. "Why would I do such an insane thing?" she asked.

"What do you think you would have been feeling if you hadn't burned yourself?" I asked again.

Mia didn't really know. "I guess I would have felt like an idiot—a real loser."

"And if you felt like a loser," I asked, "then what?" Mia shrugged. "It sounds like you think that if you have a bad feeling you have to get rid of it. Is that it?" She nodded. "Well," I said, "feelings don't have to be gotten rid of, even if they are bad feelings. In fact, your feelings are clues about things you need to pay attention to. Without our feelings to guide us, we wouldn't know how to act in life." A vacant look appeared in Mia's eyes.

"I feel like you just went away," I said. She started, realizing that she had drifted off. I pointed out that right now, here in the office, we had an opportunity to understand something important: Rather than suffer uncomfortable feelings, she blocked them out by dissociating.

"That's okay," I told her. "We all drift in and out sometimes. Just pay attention to where you went." I wanted to help her become more comfortable with her tendency to drift off and help her appreciate that her "wandering" could be a clue to a hidden pain.

"I was thinking about how I felt one summer when I went to girl scout camp and my mother was late coming up on visiting day," she finally said. I encouraged her to stay with this memory. Within a few seconds, Mia looked away. "I hate feeling like this."

"Like what?" I asked.

In a small voice, she recalled how scared and lonely she had felt waiting for her mother on a rainy Sunday in July.

"Who else knew how you felt?" I asked.

"No one." Even back then she hadn't known how to turn to others for comfort.

"I think you are a person who is very sensitive about being alone and abandoned," I said, thinking that the burning might have helped her both anesthetize and express the pain of Brett's abandonment.

And so, for the rest of the session and for many months, we explored how burning, like bulimia, serves different functions at different times. In addition to cutting and burning, nail biting, hair pulling, and pinching fall into the category of self-harm. I wanted Mia to think about the meaning of the burning for *her*.

"An act of self-harm can be a way of punishing yourself," I said, thinking aloud with her. "Or, it can give you the illusion of control at a time when you feel powerless," I added, explaining that that self-injurers sometimes can tolerate the pain that they inflict on themselves because they control it. Self-injury can also be a shock tactic, a way of reenacting some type of childhood abuse or an act of vengeance. People who let others see their wounds might be trying to communicate feelings of aggression. On the other hand, they might desperately be trying to elicit compassion. Learning how to communicate—verbally and in writing—what is going on inside is a key skill for self-injurers, as well as for the eating-disordered, because it allows them to ask for and accept the support and help of others.

Before she left my office, I gave Mia a journal. She promised that whenever she felt the impulse to harm herself, she would write about what she was feeling. Then she signed a safety contract, stating that if her feelings were still unbearable, she would call me or go to an emergency room. I've found that safety contracts work well as a kind of red flag for impulsive people like Mia. They can give a self-mutilator time to pause and reflect; I hoped that the one Mia signed would remind her that, rather than cut, she could talk to me and express herself through words. While signing a contract was no guarantee that she would never hurt herself, it was a starting point.

Telling me about burning herself was a turning point for Mia. Her job at the day care center was going well. She was now vomiting only once a day, and she and her mother were talking more. Begrudgingly, she admitted that her mother had helped her when she'd had a problem at work. Their shared experiences as teachers—something unrelated to food and weight—offered them a new connection. I felt that Mia also trusted me more and so was less inclined to run away from her problems and hide behind her wall.

I knew she had taken another step forward when she came in one day and asked, " Do dreams mean anything?" I was delighted. Mia was taking the initiative. Until now, I had done most of the asking.

She told me that for over a year she had been having a recurring dream. "In the dream I am sitting on a park bench with Brett. Suddenly my mother appears and shoves a baby in my arms. 'Take her for a while and watch her,' my mother says." The dream always ended the same way—Mia would lose the baby. In a panic, she'd search for the baby, but couldn't find it.

"What do you think it means?" I asked her.

"I'm not responsible enough."

"Responsible enough for what?"

"To be grown up, to be an adult with a baby," she replied.

"Maybe you're not ready to have a baby," I suggested. "It's hard to take care of a baby when you still have growing up to do yourself."

I explained that dreams mean many things. "What does that little baby need?" I asked.

"Someone to love it."

"Close your eyes and bring up an image of that baby. Take a good look and see it getting what it needs," I said.

Mia began to cry. "I saw my Dad pushing me in my stroller."

"Stay with that image for a moment," I suggested, but she quickly opened her eyes and looked away.

"It's too sad for me to think about what my life would have been like if he had lived," she said softly.

"See if you can sit with this image of you in your stroller for just a moment more. Let yourself go, with all your thoughts and feelings."

"I hate feeling this way," Mia said angrily. "I hate feeling so sickly and weak inside."

"Let's try an experiment," I said. "Close your eyes and float back through time. Allow yourself to go back through your life and see if you recall any other time you felt these sickly and weak feelings in your body."

"I remember being in kindergarten." In a quiet voice, Mia recalled how hard it was for her to say goodbye to her mother each morning. "I'm feeling those feelings now," she said.

"See if you can just stay with them. Let them be; see what happens if you let those feelings be present."

Mia acknowledged how uncomfortable she was. "I try not to let myself feel this way, but when I do, I realize I usually binge. And sometimes I throw up."

"You know," I said, "maybe eating, throwing up, and burning distract you from these feelings. Even though you hate throwing up, it keeps you from feeling something even harder to bear. But if you don't try to stop it, a feeling will pass on its own . . . and you'll discover that you can move on. No feeling stays with you forever."

Mia was silent. "What are you thinking?" I asked her.

"I'm thinking about that baby," she blubbered, and then quickly dried her tears and looked away.

"Can we talk about this for a minute?" I asked

"I don't have any more to say," Mia responded with her usual bravado.

"Yesterday was the first day in a *very* long time that I didn't vomit at all," Mia announced with a trace of pride at our next session. We had been working together for four and a half months. Mia had talked about everything: bingeing, vomiting, burning, friends, clothes, Brett and the ups and downs of their tumultuous relationship. Clearly, she had built up a tremendous craving to have someone really listen to her. Most recently we had talked about her mother and the new rules at home. Now, she grumbled, she was even expected to clean up after herself in the living room. Obviously, having succeeded with the bathroom, her mother had grown more comfortable allocating chores.

Mia was now taking a college course at night and writing a term paper on eating disorders. "Did you know," she said, "that Cherry Boone's family caused her anorexia?"

"What was it about her family that caused her anorexia?" I asked, curious to hear Mia's perception of the "causes" of an eating disorder—her own or Cherry Boone's.

"Well, she was influenced by deaths. She reminded me of myself. She felt like an outsider in her own family, and that's exactly how I feel." She paused. "And another thing—she kept everything inside, like I do."

I thought about a recent session where we had focused on her father's death. "It didn't really hit me until I was in sixth grade," she told me, and then recounted the story of being at a friend's home on Father's Day. "The whole family was celebrating and I felt so sad, like an outsider. It was the first time I realized I'd been cheated," she said. "And that's how I still feel—cheated. You know," she continued, "it's okay to say you feel sad or bad about your father dying, but not that you feel angry and cheated—even though that's the truth!"

"Say it again," I suggested.

She began timidly. "I'm angry at my father. Angry, angry, angry!" she said, and each time she repeated the word, her voice grew louder and louder.

"How are you feeling now?"

"Okay," she said.

"You can't believe how mean I can be to my mother, " Mia admitted during the following session. "You know, I used to say to her, 'No wonder he had a heart attack—living with you!'" It was the first time that she acknowledged feeling ashamed of how she treated her mother.

Though she was still vomiting once in a while, only once in a while is progress, too! She was becoming more insightful and grown-up, able to step back and look at her mother with more empathy. I wondered whether allowing herself to experience her legitimate anger about her father's death had opened up feelings of love for her mother.

"Losing a parent is really tough," I told her. "It's one of the most tragic losses anyone can experience. And you were only five years old—just a little older than some of the kids you care for now." I explained how young children often blame themselves when a parent dies. They feel guilty for the all the times they were angry with the parent and imagine that their anger caused the death.

"Sometimes, young children test the surviving parent," I said. "By being mean to your mother and seeing that she survived—that you didn't kill her with your meanness—you could prove to yourself that you didn't kill your dad."

Mia looked surprised at my explanation, and then grew pensive. Later she told me that she felt sad for herself, imagining what it was like for her at only five years old to lose her father.

"I guess you've kept your soft side hidden behind your wall of hostility," I said.

"I guess I am afraid to get close," she replied.

To my surprise, Mia left a message on my answering machine the following week asking if she could bring Brett, with whom she had reconciled, to one of our sessions. He did not yet know about her bulimia and burning, and I wondered how she would handle telling him. But as soon as we were gathered, Mia blurted out her secrets. Brett responded in a surprisingly gentle and caring way and requested that his name be added to her safety contract. He also came in with Mia several times over the next two months, and in one particularly moving session, revealed his own weakness—drinking too much. A few weeks later, to celebrate their two-year anniversary, they planned a one-week vacation to visit his sister in San Diego.

Mia missed her next appointment. Assuming that she was still in San Diego, I called her private line and left a message on her answering machine. No response. The next week, when she didn't show up, I grew increasingly worried that something had happened to her and left another message. After a few days with no response from her, I called her mother. Marilyn filled in the story: The day after Mia and Brett had arrived in San Diego, Brett's sister, Lara, had needed emergency surgery, and they had offered to help out with her two chil-dren. Now they were considering staying in California.

I asked Marilyn how she felt about Mia's decision. "What can I do about it?" she replied, and I felt as if we were in a time warp and back in the first session. But as we spoke, I realized that things were, indeed, different. Marilyn was much stronger now. She was accepting the fact that Mia was in charge of her life, which included living where she wanted and getting or not getting help. I thought about my last session with Mia. Perhaps bringing her boyfriend to therapy had been an even bigger step toward being grown up than I had first realized. By admit-ting him into her secret world, she had made him an ally, which caused her to be less dependent on her mother and on me.

A week later, Mia left *me* a message. "I know you will say this was impulsive and I guess you are right, but Brett and I are staying out here for now. He's tending bar and I'm hostessing. I know it's not the per-fect job for me, but it's okay for now and the weather is incredible. When I come home, I'll call you." Of course, I knew it wasn't the weather that kept her in California. But what was it? The question sat, unanswered.

I didn't know then that I would never see Mia again. Although I finally crossed her name out of my appointment book, I would think of her on many subsequent Thursday afternoons, and my emotions would rise and sink.

On the one hand, I felt angry: How could she do this to herself—to me? Walk away from her job, her school, *our* relationship—how could she throw them all away so easily? And I felt uneasy. She still had bulimic episodes; working in a restaurant and being around food made her vulnerable. Although she had let me see behind her wall, I wasn't sure that Mia had developed a strong enough connection with herself to handle the inevitable stresses of life without taking refuge in bingeing, vomiting, or burning. I do know that until recovery is deeply embedded, the risk of relapse looms.

On the other hand, I felt hopeful. Mia had made great progress in many areas. Whether or not this was the right job for her, she was working. Her bingeing and vomiting episodes had significantly decreased, and since signing the contract with me months earlier, she apparently hadn't burned herself. Her relationships with her mother and Brett were vastly improved. She had begun to feel more comfortable about looking at her life and accepting the pain that had been a part of it. In the space of seven months of therapy, Mia had broken free from the place in which she was stuck and started her journey to maturity. I hoped that she would take what she had learned about herself in my office and expand on it as she built her new life.

We tend to expect people's stories to resolve neatly, like the stories we see in movies and on TV. We look for miraculous recoveries and cathartic experiences. Real lives aren't like that. We grow by taking small, uneven steps, backward and forward. We might take a giant step, but with the possibility of unfinished business left behind. Indeed, Mia had left therapy with a lot of healing still undone.

Nevertheless, I reminded myself that there are other ways to heal and grow up besides being in therapy. Certainly, starting a new life in a new town with her boyfriend would stretch her, and I know from my own life and the lives of my patients that with each stretch, we grow. My work as a therapist has shown me that every time somebody has a healing moment, that experience lodges deep within, and their sense of self expands to include the notion, *I can heal*. While Mia might go back to her old ways of coping in the face of stress or trauma, her knowledge that she had taken risks and overcome "bad habits" would, I hoped, help her bounce back when adversity hit.

Just a month ago, I was waiting at red light, listening to classical music, when suddenly I caught sight of a young woman about Mia's age and build, who was wearing a t-shirt printed with the words, "If you hate loud music, you must be old!" She stepped off the curb and crossed the street directly in front of my car. Once again, Mia came to mind.

As the light changed and I drove away, I thought about how much I had wanted her story to have a happy ending—resolved and complete. I would have to accept that this wasn't how it was going to be . . . at least for now. To be sure, we had discovered enough cracks for her to dismantle part of her wall and build a deeper connection to herself and others—her mother, the father she'd lost, Brett, and me. But I would simply have to face the fact that, like all real stories about growth, Mia's was still a work in progress.

3

Joy Shared, Twice the Gain, Sorrow Shared, Half the Pain

All suffering is bearable if it is seen as part of a story.
—Isak Dinesen

"You won't believe what I'm going to tell you!" Estelle announced as she walked into my office with a wide smile on her face. "It's the first full week—no bingeing and no *vomiting!*"

We had met eight months earlier on a September morning I would long remember. It was the first day of the new school year. For me and my children, the morning was filled with the inevitable excitement and tensions of a new chapter in life. That day was memorable for another reason: It marked the one-month anniversary of my husband's moving out. We had been married for 15 years.

Although the weather was unusually warm, I was shivering when the yellow school buses picked up 12-year-old Zach and his 8-year-old sister, Rachel. "Bye, Mom." Walking back down my street, a wave of exhaustion washed over me. Once home, I realized how overwhelmed I was and considered climbing back into bed, an uncharacteristic move. A ringing phone disrupted this option. It was Estelle, a prospective patient.

In a high-pitched, urgent voice she bombarded me with questions about therapy. She had heard that I was an expert on eating disorders. Was that true? Did I deal with her problem, bulimia? And how long did therapy take, usually?

Suddenly, my exhaustion evaporated. How remarkably resilient we can be, I thought, relieved that the competent psychologist in me had not disappeared in the midst of my emotional tornado. "I can't really answer your questions without meeting you and hearing more about your problem," I told Estelle, and suggested that we set up a consultation.

"Will you tell me if you think I'm hopeless?" She paused. "I've never been in therapy and I've heard it takes years! I'm 58 years old," she warned me emphatically, "not young anymore."

Fifty-eight years old! Until recently I had considered bulimia primarily an adolescent epidemic, but within the past few months several women in their 30's and 40's had called me. Was the epidemic spreading? Had Estelle been struggling for a long time or had her problem just developed? I hoped that it hadn't been with her for a lifetime, because the more chronic, the more difficult eating disorders are to heal. In either case, I had never worked with a bulimic patient of this age. My mind raced, but I kept my nagging questions on the back burner and refocused my attention on our conversation.

"That's really the point of the consultation," I said. "If I think I can help you, I'll let you know how we might best work together. And if I can't, I'll let you know that, too. You'll have a chance to get a sense of whether or not you want to work with me, as well. Can we set up an appointment for this Wednesday morning at ten o'clock?"

I deliberately defined our first meeting as only a consultation to protect us both from making a premature commitment. Selecting a therapist is never easy, and Estelle was new to therapy. People who have never been in treatment tend to choose a therapist based on qualifications, and only during the first meeting do they realize how important is the "fit." It's like a blind date: However perfect the profile sounds, once two people face each other across the dinner table, chemistry becomes everything.

At ten o'clock Wednesday morning, I opened the door to my waiting room and was greeted by an attractive woman in a pink warm-up suit. "Hi!" she said cheerily. I felt as if I was meeting someone at a cocktail party. She had begun speaking even before she sat down in my office. "I'm a full-time administrator of a successful business, an owner of two homes and a slave to a busy social calendar. But now, after running my *entire* life without a therapist," she said, tossing her curly red hair with dramatic flair, "something has happened."

"What is that?"

"My life has finally caught up with me." Her voice was strong, but her eyes avoided mine.

"Your life has 'finally caught up with you,'" I repeated, confused. "Could you tell me what you mean by that?"

"I guess I'm just overwhelmed," she said. The fact that she described herself with the very word I had been using to describe myself a few days earlier did not escape me. "It's not that we haven't had our share of trouble. But no one in our family has ever seen a therapist."

"Perhaps we can begin with your family," I suggested. "What can you tell me about them?"

"Here's the low-down," she said, as if we were best of friends already. "I have two children who really aren't children anymore. Alan, the oldest, is 36. He's a successful optometrist. He and his wife, Wendy, live in Dallas with their 7-year-old, Elyssa, who was born with a cleft palate. And my daughter, Heddy—she's a year younger than Alan—is an attorney. She's divorced from the biggest bastard in the world! He left her with two boys who are now five and six, but when he walked out, they were babies. Adorable, but difficult! They gave new meaning to the term "Wild Indians!" The three of them have just moved in with me and Jerry. He's my husband. We'll be married 37 years this July. What do you think of that?" She took a breath and stopped talking. "Anything else you want to know?"

Given that she had come in to talk about her bulimia, I was struck by Estelle's superficial tone. *Is she so ashamed about her eating disorder that she wants to impress me with the normal life she has led as a mother and wife?* I wondered.

"Even though lots of my friends have spent years on therapists' couches, it never even occurred to me to see someone. I just never had a need. I guess I've worked things out for myself, as best I could. I never *thought* about seeing a shrink—you don't mind if I call you a shrink?"

Grinning at her spunkiness, I nodded and encouraged her to continue. This was a woman who presented herself as competent and self-assertive, at least on the surface. I wondered if she would have greater difficulty when it came to revealing her inner life, for people with bulimia tend to be disconnected from their emotions. This difficulty, in fact, lies at the heart of their problem.

"My life was always problem-free, you might say, until now," she said. Again, she seemed to skim the surface of her emotional life: *Who amongst us has a problem-free life?* I wondered.

"Until now?" I asked. Now, she informed me, her life was out of control. "What is out of control?"

"My weight is out of control," she said, "and so is my bulimia."

"So your life, your weight, and your bulimia are out of control," I repeated, pleased that she had paved the way for us to explore the connection between her life and her bulimia. I wanted to help Estelle become aware that obsessing about weight loss is a way of not thinking about something that is going on in your life—something you can't cope with. In other words, eating disorders are not about being thin; they're a coping strategy. The question that Estelle needed to start asking herself was what was she trying *not* to think about? What, in her life, was so painful that she could only cope by shutting herself down? With some people, this awareness takes months to develop, but with Estelle, the opportunity to look at this connection presented itself right away.

"Do you have any idea why everything is out of control, *now?*" I asked her. I emphasized the word now because it is by paying attention to the present moment that insight is born. My question hung heavily in the air. I wondered if she was summoning up the courage to reveal her thoughts, but I was off-base.

"Where should I begin?" she asked.

"Wherever you think it could be helpful to start," I replied.

She hesitated. "I don't know what you want to know."

"Perhaps you might begin by telling me about your bulimia."

Estelle pursed her lips and shrugged her shoulders, communicating a clear message, "Keep away!" Although experience has taught me that only by staying with the details of her eating disorder would we journey to the depths of her problem, I sensed her uneasiness. I imagined that she was not comfortable enough to talk about the details—yet.

"Where should I begin?" she asked again. As we sat in the quiet on the edge of the unknown journey we were about to take, I feared we were getting stuck already. Estelle might need to feel safer with me before she could open up, so I decided to take the lead and address how she felt about being personal with me.

"Before we get to the bulimia . . . How was it for you to come here today?"

Estelle looked like she was trying to hold back her tears. "You have no idea how hard it was," she managed to say.

"But you came," I said, and paused for a moment. "How did you make that decision?"

Her words came out in a barely audible whisper. "I've been bulimic for 14 years and I can't take it anymore."

After we had worked together for several sessions, I understood why it was so tough for Estelle to open up. She was raised in a family with two rules: Silence is Golden, and Honor your Father and Mother. She had learned from her parents that [roblems are a sign of weakness and people don't like to hear about them. This also explained why it was so difficult for her to admit to herself or anyone else that she had a problem and needed therapy. In fact, the decision to see me had actually come from her family, who had pushed her into making the appointment after discovering what Estelle referred to as her "dirty secret."

In a later family therapy session, Estelle's daughter told me how she had learned the truth about her mother. A hurricane warning had closed Heddy's office early. Upon arriving home, she immediately knew something was wrong. Her first hint was the coffee table. Ordinarily tidy, it was strewn with half-empty dishes, empty boxes, and candy wrappers. The second sign was Estelle dozing on the couch. Heddy hadn't seen her mother napping during the day for two decades. One section of the local newspaper was spread across her chest; the remainder was scattered across the floor—odd, since Estelle was meticulous and always kept the newspapers piled neatly under the coffee table. Leaving her mother asleep on the couch, Heddy went into the kitchen to get a glass of water. When she saw the unusual state of disarray, she knew that her mother was in trouble.

Heddy admitted that she had been suspicious for months. Not only were Estelle's attitudes towards food and eating alarming—she was a picky eater who rarely ate with the family, the refrigerator was either overflowing or empty, she made grocery lists obsessively and shopped at odd hours, usually late at night—but she was also distant and seemed unusually preoccupied. All this had left Heddy with a sense of foreboding, so the scene greeting her that day was the final tip-off.

The next night, Heddy spoke with her father, and together they sat Estelle down and voiced their concern. Estelle was adamant—nothing was wrong! But neither Heddy nor Jerry would back down. That weekend, Alan and Wendy flew in for a family discussion.

I heard Estelle's version of the story during our first session. The way she remembered it, she had been confronted. All she could remember was that she had felt numb, frozen. She barely spoke up, while the others talked nonstop, assaulting her with their suspicions. Eventually Estelle broke down crying. The secret was out.

"*They* are really the reason I'm here," Estelle said. "I didn't want to come, but I couldn't say no, especially to Heddy! She was devastated. My son, too. They kept insisting I call someone, and eventually, I caved in. Heddy got your number from our family physician. So here I am!" Her somber mood vanished, and in a light-hearted, almost joking way, she repeated: "So here I am . . . help!"

I faltered, searching for a response. Estelle was asking for help, but at the same time, she was telling me that she didn't want it. I felt uneasy, for people often don't get better in therapy when they're trying to meet someone else's agenda. It's hard enough for a person to change when they really want to.

"You probably can't help me," Estelle said, echoing my worst fear. Her voice had shifted and now sounded almost confrontational.

"That's what we're here to figure out together," I said, wanting to emphasize that our success was dependent not only on my expertise, but on her willingness to be an active participant in a collaboration. "Why don't you begin by telling me about how *you* see the problems that have brought you here today?"

"I can tell you one thing. Bulimia is a filthy habit," she replied, suddenly agitated, "and I must be totally crazy, out of my mind to be bingeing and getting rid of my food."

"I doubt you're crazy," I said. "In fact, I suspect you had some pretty good reasons to begin bingeing." I wanted her to understand that there's always a good reason for everything we do, even things that are destructive, and even when we think we must be crazy.

"I must have 'good' reasons to binge and get rid of my food?" she paused. "Of course I do, I don't want to be fat!" Her response hardly surprised me, for like most people with eating problems, Estelle was unaware that purging allowed her to get rid of not only her excess food, but her intolerable feelings as well.

"So *one* good reason," I said, joining in her definition of the problem, "is that you don't want to be fat." Estelle nodded vigorously, and I felt our relationship back on solid ground. "Tell me about that," I said.

"Well, I wasn't going to talk about this, but just last night, I had a major, out-of-control binge." Estelle lowered her voice before continuing. "No one would believe what I ate. Like a vacuum, I attacked the refrigerator, sucking up whatever was in sight. No kidding. Half a lemon meringue pie, a pint of vanilla ice cream, a box of Oreos and some crackers and cheese—in less than an hour they were gone." She had felt sick and full of self-loathing afterwards.

"Do you always vomit after a binge?" I asked.

Estelle rolled her eyes. Clearly I was an idiot. "Don't you think I'd be even bigger than I am if I didn't vomit?" For Estelle, a purge *always* followed a binge.

"What about laxatives? Diuretics?"

"God, no!" Estelle exclaimed. "Thank God I don't do that! Just vomiting." She spontaneously volunteered more information. "In the beginning, I hardly ever vomited."

"And now, how often?" I asked.

"I don't know," she said. "I never thought about it."

"Well," I said, "If you take a moment and think about it, how often do you think you binge and vomit? Once a day? A week? After every meal?"

She gazed at me with a blank look on her face. "I really don't know," she finally said. "Is it important for me to know?"

"Yes," I said, "And I'll tell you why. All of us have different kinds of hungers. Sometimes we eat when we're hungry for food. And sometimes we eat when our hungers are emotional. Have you ever thought about it in this way?"

Estelle shrugged. "I really haven't."

"It's important to pay attention to your eating habits," I said. "They probably have a lot to tell you. Eating when you're hungry is different than eating when you're not."

Estelle's long silence made me nervous. Had I gone too fast again?

"This must be really hard," I said, "talking about all these details."

"It is hard," she said. "You are the first person I've ever told. I never thought we'd be talking about the details of my bulimia, but it's actually easier than I thought it would be."

"You have a lot of courage," I said. "Do you know how it began?"

"Yes," she replied quickly. I was skeptical, for it is extremely difficult to "know" how complex problems begin, but I was curious about how she saw her situation. "My daughter was getting married," she went on, "and I wanted to lose weight before the wedding."

"Tell me about it."

She wanted to fit into a size 10 dress. She set a limit of only a thousand calories a day, but the weight didn't come off fast enough. She cut her calories to 900. Then 800. At 700 calories a day, she started losing weight, but the process was interminably slow. And although she was finally getting slimmer, she was always hungry. So she began to binge.

At first the binges consisted of healthy food. She consumed huge quantities of steamed vegetables. On one particularly bad day, Estelle recalled, she polished off 14 bunches of broccoli, which made her sick. Cramps and nausea were followed by horrible bouts of diarrhea. Had I ever heard of that? I assured her that I had.

"Most people are conflicted about diarrhea," I said. "On the one hand, they are physically debilitated by the cramping and water loss. The dehydration really knocks you out. Did that happen to you?" She nodded, and I continued. "On the other hand, people are secretly delighted because they think that having diarrhea means they won't gain weight. Did you ever feel that way?" Again, she nodded. "Unfortunately, that's a myth," I said, explaining that weight lost through dehydration is dangerous and quickly regained.

After the broccoli phase came artichokes. "I'd buy, steam, and eat a dozen at a time."

"It must take a long time to eat a dozen artichokes," I said. She agreed.

Her craving for vegetables transformed into uncontrollable fruit binges. A dozen Florida oranges sent by Aunt Ruthie were consumed in one day. Oranges led to grapefruits and then to tangerines. Next, her sweet tooth took over. Mars Bars and licorice became enemy number one. Her routine expanded to fast-food places: daily stops at the 7-Eleven for potato chips and other binge foods, with a box of sugar-covered donuts from the local bakery as the grand finale. Naturally, she began to gain weight. As the scale climbed, she became consumed by her fear of fat, but paradoxically, she found that food calmed her down.

"I was caught in a vicious cycle. I didn't know how to get free." I knew, of course, the cycle to which she was referring. Feeling out of control is depressing. To cope with depression, she turned to food, which shamed her. She stopped talking to people and felt lonely, and then ate to soothe her loneliness. Thus began the cycle of bulimia that had persisted for more than a decade. She never believed it would become so deeply entrenched that she could not stop. She certainly never imagined that the final scene would be a showdown with her daughter.

Although it was bulimia that had forced her to seek help, it was not her bulimia that Estelle wanted to change. What she wanted was to lose weight. Could I help her with that? The vomiting wasn't working anymore. And she couldn't stop eating compulsively, especially this past year, which had been particularly bad.

"Bad?" I asked.

"Bad!" she exclaimed, for she had been gaining, gaining, gaining! How she had gained these last 16 pounds was incomprehensible! And inexcusable! In her opinion, 16 disgusting pounds of fat were the only problem.

I had a different opinion. "For 14 years you have stuffed down your feelings with food. You have numbed and medicated yourself. You have lost touch with your appetites, hungers, and desires," I said, specifically using metaphors to evoke the connection between food and feelings. "For 14 years you have lived with a secret that has made you feel ashamed, and the shame has kept you lonely and withdrawn." But I could not budge Estelle. Her definition of the problem was that her bulimia had stopped "working."

"Why do you think it stopped working?" I finally asked. She didn't know. "What has been going on this past year?"

In response to this simple question, a deluge of facts poured forth. Devastating losses had ravaged her family in a short period of time. First her mother had died, two years earlier. "At 89, her time had come,"

Estelle said in a matter-of-fact manner. One month later, her older brother, Leon, died. "These deaths were expected," she said, discounting the importance of her loss. "After all, Leon was 11 years older than me, and people don't live forever!" However, it was the sudden death of her younger brother, Joey, the previous year, that had left her completely devastated.

"Tell me about Joey."

Estelle remained silent. Finally she said, "I can't. And anyway, what's the point?"

Talking is healing, so, to draw her in, I said, "You have had so much loss and so much pain."

"Life *is* pain," she agreed, "but who, besides you, whom I am paying, wants to hear about it?"

"What did you do with your pain after Joey was gone?" I was learning to disregard her dismissals.

She shrugged. "People don't like to hear about your troubles," she said.

I tried again. "With whom did you cry?"

"We're not big criers in our family," she said proudly. "We're fighters who have strength and courage."

This was how our relationship began: Two people, with two different agendas and ideas about life, attempting to forge a connection.

"I almost didn't come back," Estelle said, opening the second session. "You can't imagine how many times I thought of calling and leaving you a message that I had changed my mind." I wasn't surprised. She must have realized that therapy is about revealing one's innermost self. The decision to commit isn't easy, especially for individuals with bulimia, who are more used to reaching out to food than to people.

"You told me that you are from a family of fighters who don't give up. I'm curious—what drew you back?" I asked.

"I have another secret," she admitted sheepishly. "But even though I made a commitment to tell you what's going on, it's a lot harder than I thought it would be! What's the point of coming here if I can't be honest?"

"It sounds as if you're in a Catch-22," I said. "You want to trust me, but you're afraid you'll regret opening up. But, if you don't open up, you'll regret not taking the chance." Good therapy requires both safety and risk-taking, and I hoped I was helping her properly balance the two. We spent much of the session exploring these ambivalent feelings. Perhaps simply talking about them freed her, for as the session was about to end, she took a leap and told me about Richard.

Estelle had met Richard 15 years earlier. What began as an office friendship quickly evolved into an affair, and for 12 years they were lovers. With him she found a unique emotional connection. Even after their love affair was over, Richard remained a daily presence in her life and continued to occupy a cherished place in her heart as well.

"Not a day goes by that he isn't on my mind." She sighed and continued, "Remember the day of the hurricane when Heddy found me passed out on the couch? I didn't tell you the whole story. After I got home from work, I was browsing through the newspapers and a headline stopped me." A freak accident on the interstate involving three vehicles had left seven people dead, one of whom was Richard. Staring at the obituary, she was unable to digest the words, the image, his photograph, his death. Unimaginable, unbearable.

"How did you bear the unbearable?" I wondered aloud, feeling her pain.

"All I remember was sitting on the couch thinking, 'This is too horrible, too unfair. I'm not going to make it.' And suddenly, I was in the kitchen in front of the refrigerator gazing at the food on the shelves."

"You are reading the paper, you are destroyed by Richard's death," I said slowly, "and suddenly, you are in front of the refrigerator." Estelle nodded, apparently blind to the connection she had made between her emotional pain and her reflexive bingeing. I invited her to join me in a meditation so we could relive that horrific moment together. "Take a breath, and if you are comfortable, allow your eyes to close. Let's go back to the moment you were sitting on the couch, reading the paper. That headline has just caught your eye. See yourself reading the news. Allow yourself to be with all your feelings and sensations as you recall and absorb this tragedy. See yourself making your way from the couch to the refrigerator. Are you with me?" Eyes closed, Estelle nodded.

"Let me sit with you in front of the refrigerator," I said, joining in her struggle. We sat in the quiet, and I imagined myself with Estelle, on a stool, in front of her open refrigerator. "What are you feeling?" I finally asked. Estelle shrugged. "What is your shrug saying?"

"I know I *should* feel sad," she said, "and I suppose that somewhere inside, I am heartbroken. But right now, I feel nothing. I'm numb."

This was how our second session ended.

Estelle spent the next several sessions talking about the 14 years she and Richard had met regularly on Thursday afternoons at the Mont Blanc Hotel. "You know, I never thought about it, but Richard and I became involved right before Heddy announced her engagement." Her eyes widened when we explored this coincidence: Maybe the onset of her starving had more to do with her shame around her secret affair than wanting to fit into the dress for Heddy's wedding.

Next we discussed Estelle's marriage. Although it had been unsatisfying for years, she hadn't wanted to break up her family, even after meeting Richard, and especially right before her daughter's wedding. For 12 years, their relationship grew and thrived. How eagerly she had looked forward to their time together!

"It may sound like I'm exaggerating, but we were perfect for each other." In a way she had never anticipated, she was drawn to his laughter, his fears, and to the closeness that he offered. "He listened to me." His predictable line of farewell, "Time flies when you're having fun!" stretched out their endless goodbyes. One last hug, an extra touch, a lingering kiss, but finally, the inevitable parting.

She paid a terrible price. Once in her car, a vicious inner dialogue began: *You are having an affair. You are committing adultery. What a dirty word. What a disgusting person you are. A liar, a cheat, a sneak. Stop it now! No more rendezvous with Richard. Call him and tell him it's over! But how could I leave Richard? My marriage has been bleak for decades. It's Jerry I should leave. Divorce—what an ugly concept! No divorces in our family! People just stick it out. We are fighters—that's who we are! We honor our commitments.*

Before long, she would sink into a bottomless, black hole. In the hour-long drive home, she found only one way to save herself. By the time she pulled into the garage, the floor of her car was covered with tear-soaked tissues and the remnants of her binges: empty wrappers from Mars Bars, licorice candy, and donuts. She was grateful that Jerry played racketball on Thursday nights and didn't get home until she was asleep. His absence freed her from confronting her guilt; the binges freed her from confronting her longing for Richard. Sickened, tired, and numb, she would pass out on her bed.

Listening to Estelle, I was near tears. She, however, remained dry-eyed—distanced from her feelings, her story, and me. "How is it for you now, to tell me about these feelings?" I asked when this particularly moving session drew to a close.

"What feelings?" Estelle asked, but the quiver in her voice suggested to me that she was getting closer to them.

Over the next few months, we pieced together the story of a marriage that had withered from years of neglect. Both Estelle and Jerry had grown up learning to keep things on an even keel. Neither of them rocked the boat, and this lack of communication left Estelle feeling parched and famished. In contrast to the deadness of her marriage, Richard filled her hunger for intimacy, contact, and connection. "How hungry we were for one another," she mused thoughtfully. Identifying her inner hungers grew into a major theme of our work together.

Eventually her routine with Richard stabilized. Thursdays was the Mont Blanc Hotel. Monday and Wednesday mornings they had long talks on the phone. Weekends were excruciatingly long. Their time together became the centerpiece of her life.

One June evening, after she and Richard had been together for 12 years, Estelle's world suddenly collapsed. Richard had returned home to an empty apartment. His wife, Madeline, had departed abruptly, leaving only a note: "I'm sure you won't be disappointed to find me gone. Our marriage has been dying for years. We each deserve more."

Later, he learned that she and a lover had fled to Arizona. Richard was suddenly free, and his freedom upset the delicate balance that he and Estelle had created. Thursdays at the Mont Blanc no longer sufficed for Richard; he was lonely and needed more contact than Estelle could offer. Incessantly, he begged her to leave Jerry. Loving pleas became bitter arguments. Finally he gave up.

"I don't want to abandon you," he explained, insisting that they could remain friends. After a torturous ending to their affair, he met, and eventually married another woman, but he and Estelle had remained in touch until his death, the shock of which had triggered her fateful binge.

"It sounds like Richard fed a deep place in you," I said one day, reiterating what I had tried to help her see many times before. This time Estelle's reaction was different. She began to sob. Her tears dislodged another barrier that had protected her from knowing the depths of her pain.

I had been waiting for these tears since Estelle's first session, when she told me, "I'm not really a crier." Crying, as babies know, is a natural way of calling out for comfort when something hurts; Estelle, coming from a family that considered emotional neediness a sign of weakness, had learned to distract herself from pain rather than depend on others for solace. This kept her isolated from her feelings, and from her family, as well. Connections, after all, are basic to human survival and pleasure. Likewise, to feel is the essence of being alive; joy, sorrow, disappointment, surprise, all make human experience rich. I wanted Estelle, who had shut out sorrow and with it joy, to understand how important her pain really was. Her tears were a beginning.

Bulimia always develops for a reason. Previously, Estelle had perceived that her weight and eating disorder were the primary sources of her pain. Once she became aware that her bulimia masked and expressed a deeper suffering, an inner dialogue began: *There is something wrong inside that can't be fixed by eating steamed vegetables...Or by losing 2, 5 or 10 pounds...Or even by wearing size 8...What is it?*

One night she dreamed that she was lost in a thick forest, search-ing for something to eat. She came upon a scarecrow in a cornfield. Ravenously, she pulled the ears of corn from the husks, but stopped when she realized that the kernels were brown, inedible pellets, dried up by the sun. This dream made clear that her suffering was not due to her weight, but to an inner emptiness. She had lost the love of her life but had sought to regain a sense of wholeness in a number on the scale.

Months passed. We explored the ways in which her obsession with food and weight had numbed her from experiencing the frustration and disappointment that relationships often bring. It had initially anesthetized her from feeling rage at a husband who had ignored and neglected her, and later from feeling ashamed at betraying her husband by committing adultery. It also protected her from experienc-ing the pain of Richard's loss.

As Estelle began to pay more attention to how she felt, her disor-dered eating receded and she relaxed her vigilance over what she ate and weighed. "What am I hungry for now?" she would frequently ask herself both in and out of sessions. She paid more attention to her internal life, and her daily existence took on a richer meaning. She began listening more carefully to herself when she spoke with her husband, when she drove to my office, when we sat together. She developed a deeper connection to her hungry self, a self that craved being listened to and validated. Over time, she began to experience human relationships as a source of joy and comfort, while *our* relation-ship nourished her courage to look within.

Identifying the negatives in our relationship became the next arena for growth. I wanted her to understand that relationships can with-stand differences, and that, contrary to what her parents had taught, she could express her displeasure instead of meekly abiding by other people's agendas. If she saw that our relationship was able to survive the waves, I reasoned, she would gain more confidence to rock the boat with others. Eventually, giving voice to what felt right on the inside, instead of what looked right on the outside, might help her to live more spontaneously.

So one day I asked her, "Doesn't anything about me ever bother you?" With a bit of prodding on my part, she admitted that she didn't like my standard "shrink" question, "How did that make you feel?" It had always irked her, but she had been reluctant to bring it up and risk losing me. During the weeks that followed, I encouraged her to pay more attention to the ways I differed from her, even disappointed her. As I watched her express genuine feelings instead of worrying about pleasing me, I was reminded that true healing comes from paying attention to the heart and taking risks.

Her personal relationships expanded in baby steps. One day she came into my office beaming. She had gone out for lunch with Rose, a co-worker. For years their relationship had been filled with monotonous small talk, but yesterday, Estelle had taken the plunge and told Rose about her eating disorder. In response, Rose revealed her battle with alcoholism. That day they returned to the office an hour later than usual and with a closer bond.

Estelle and I had been working together several months when I thought about inviting her to join a new bulimia group that I was starting, even though her age concerned me. Would a 58-year-old woman fit in with women in their 20's and 30's? Or would their disparate ages and life stages present an insurmountable barrier?

"Group therapy is different from individual sessions, " I said. When a group works well, people are able to spontaneously relate in a way that is both authentic and healing. "Speaking with others about your life and your bulimia will help you, I believe."

As I spoke, Estelle looked away. "Group? Why would you think I would want to join a group?" she asked angrily. "Don't you remember how difficult is was for me to come see you? Why would I want to share my bulimia with strangers?"

I had stepped into another dark hole. I did appreciate her need for privacy; I was aware that the only reason she had come to therapy was because she didn't want to burden her daughter or husband. Nevertheless, I reminded her that even though our relationship had strengthened, some of her bulimic symptoms still remained. This didn't surprise me, for a few months of therapy can hardly compete with a 14-year habit.

"Group therapy has a way of helping people free themselves from stuck places," I persisted. "Other people's stories provide new windows for us to understand our own." The positive energy between us began to evaporate. Her furrowed brow and body language warned me, *Back off, Jude.* "I'm losing you," I said.

"No group for me." She shook her head as if to toss me off. "I don't think so."

"You don't think so," I repeated, attempting to weather this uncomfortable moment, reminding myself that people grow by repairing ruptures. If we could repair this one, perhaps she would be able to eventually transfer this resiliency into the rest of her life.

Estelle remained silent, unresponsive. "You're still wondering, why a group?" I said, and as I spoke, I wondered how I could be respectful of who she was while helping her take the risk and join. How could I convey my deepest beliefs about relationships, relatedness, and healing? I was silent, waiting, and out of the silence, an answer emerged. "I'll tell you why a group," I said. "It may sound like I'm switching subjects, but I'm not. Let me tell you a story."

The past weekend was Yom Kippur, the holiest day in the Jewish year, and I had attended synagogue. The sanctuary was so very peaceful; the quiet, calming. Absorbed in the spacious grandeur, the rich notes of the organ filled my heart. Exquisite in their simplicity, huge white lilies hugged the altar. The sunlight pouring through the stained glass windows was breathtaking. I found myself examining the windows, each of which had a biblical quote. One was particularly memorable—so memorable that I wrote it down. I thought it might speak to Estelle.

"May I?" I asked. She nodded. I opened my pocketbook, took out the wrinkled piece of paper, and read:

> *Joy shared, twice the gain,*
> *Sorrow shared, half the pain.*

"That's beautiful," she said.

"I think so, too," I said. "It's from Psalms. Do you know why I read it to you?" She didn't. "Because it speaks about the healing qualities of sharing. You are a woman who has a lot of pain. To protect yourself, you've kept it locked in your body, and you've isolated yourself. Words are hard for you, but you need to express your pain in words, especially now, when you're mourning. You need to be heard. In the Jewish religion, when someone dies, we have a *minyan*," I said, referring to the requirement that a minimum number of people be present for a mourning service. "The wisdom of our ancestors taught that sharing grief is healing. That's why you should join the group."

At first she was quiet. Then she asked me to repeat the quote so that she could write it down. When she read it aloud, her voice quivered and her eyes filled with tears. "It's beautiful," she said. "Hearing you talk made me think of things I haven't thought of in years. I'm remembering my father. I loved going to church with him when I was young. He died 20 years ago and just now, I thought about him and felt like crying. You are making me think of him in a different way." A new phase of therapy began as Estelle became more able to open her heart to grief, loss, and her yearning for love.

When she returned the following week, Estelle said, "I read that quote to my husband." That had really surprised her, because she rarely discussed personal things with anyone, especially him. "He was very moved. It made me feel a lot closer to him." She told him about the therapy group, and he encouraged her to join, which further amazed her.

Two years later, when our final session was drawing to a close, Estelle asked, "Do you remember that quote you gave me before I joined the group?" I nodded. She had put a copy of it on the door of her refrigerator. It helped to remind her that when she felt overwhelmed with feelings, she didn't have to eat. She could turn to people instead.

"I'm still not very good at it," she said, but she was trying. Just this past week she had renewed her contact with cousin Millie, who lived only minutes away. I thought about how *our* relationship had served as a stepping stone, enabling her to feel safe enough to reach out and expand her connections to others.

Standing in the doorway of my office, she paused. She had one last thing to say. "I'm glad you remember the quote," she said. I assured her that I not only recalled the quote, but the exact moment I had given it to her. What, I wondered, was next?

"I told you about the copy on my refrigerator, but I've kept the original in my bag all this time." She opened her purse, unzipped the inner pocket, and pulled out the original, wrinkled scrap of paper that had been with her these past two years. Our eyes met, and in that moment I became acutely aware of what I had meant to her, what she had meant to me, and how much I would miss her. A lump grew in my throat, and my eyes filled with tears.

"Thank you for showing me," I said, and then she tucked the paper back into her pocketbook, zipped it closed, turned, and left.

Estelle's question echoed in the quiet. *Did I remember giving her the piece of paper?* Of course I remembered, for when we are truly present in our work, we are touched by what happens there. It is precisely because I *was* touched by her in a unique way that I had reached within myself. Her ache had evoked an ache of mine. A memory emerged:

> *It is Yom Kippur morning. I am sitting in the synagogue with sun streaming through the stained glass windows that touch and inspire me. Although I am between my two children, I feel more alone than I have felt in years, for I have recently separated from my husband, the father of my children. This is the first holiday I face alone. Tears threaten to erupt. Feeling overwhelmed, I search wildly for calm, and my eyes fall on those stained glass windows, on the words from Psalms that will weave themselves into my heartstrings and, eventually, into Estelle's, too.*

This memory reminded me that my own wounds can be a source of connection that enhance rather than hamper my capacity to understand and empathize with my patients. Although Estelle never asked, and I never volunteered to explain the circumstances surrounding this piece of paper, the fact that I had it contained many messages. Certainly it told her that I was a person who was familiar with loss and grief. As opposed to a silent expert, I offered myself as a collaborator, one who was willing to share my personal experiences and strategies for growth.

For better or worse, psychotherapy is a deeply personal relationship. Estelle's words echoed: "*I carried the piece of paper in my pocketbook.*" Automatically I translated her words into my language, the language of feelings. She had carried me in her heart, and I felt privileged that she had done so, for feeling that I make a difference in the life of another person, whether that person is my child, my friend, my husband, or my patient, is an invigorating and sacred experience.

When I think about Estelle standing at the door, I am reminded of a simple but profound lesson: Not only do therapists strive to heal patients, but our work enables us to revisit and repair what needs healing in ourselves. By honoring my intuitive sense and staying open to my own experience, I was able to forge a unique and sturdy bond with Estelle. Finally, by being more personal, I took a risk. Estelle grew, and so did I.

4

The Eye of the Hurricane

*In the midst of winter, I finally learned in me
there was an invincible summer.*
—ALBERT CAMUS

"This therapy is no different than the others—a big, fat failure, just like me," Elinor said, throwing herself into the chair. "I considered not coming here today. In fact, maybe this should be our last session." Her words chilled my heart. We had been working together for three months, and everything was going well, but now, she seemed serious about quitting therapy. Slumped over, Elinor looked as if she had lost all hope.

"I've done it again!" she moaned. "I had another one of those damned out-of-control rampages. And I was stupid enough to think that I was through abusing myself with food. What a jerk! Non-stop eating like a pig. That's me, all right—a pig!"

This latest binge was worse than any before, because it had happened in public. That morning at her daughter's playgroup, Elinor had stuffed herself mercilessly in front of her three-year-old daughter, Meri, and the other mothers—all neighborhood friends who knew nothing about her lifetime problem with compulsive eating. "I must have looked repulsive, reaching and grabbing. Repulsive!" Her voice reached a shrill crescendo, "And in front of a roomful of people!"

"Elinor," I said, interrupting her self-attacking harangue, "can you slow down and tell me what happened?"

"Slow down? I don't think so," she said, glaring at me. "You can't imagine how disgusting I must have looked. How gross I felt."

"Just a minute," I said. "Take a breath and see if you can tell me exactly what happened."

"What happened?" Her voice rose another octave. "I haven't a clue! Mindless eating, that's what *you* would call it. And after coming here and paying you all this money."

I cringed. Her meaning was clear: *You and your mindful eating philosophy can drop dead!* At least she was no longer attacking *herself*— that was a sign of progress. Maybe I should be pleased. But I didn't feel at all pleased. In fact, I was worried. She was fed up and felt like a failure, and, in her eyes, so was I. A week earlier she had respected and admired me because she was on the mend. But now, she held me responsible for her most recent binge, even though early on I had warned her that relapse was a predictable part of recovery. I wasn't helping her, "not that I expected much help anyway," she reminded me. "Perhaps this should be our last session," she repeated. Her hopelessness felt contagious. I struggled against being swept into her despair. Little did we know that we were sitting on the edge of a breakthrough.

Elinor had first called two days before New Year's Eve. Her voice was hesitant and barely audible. "It's my weight. I can't stand myself anymore," she said, as if she was forcing herself to utter these shameful words. "I just made my New Year's resolution. This is the year I'm going to get my eating under control. Do you have any openings?"

I had anticipated meeting a shy, heavy woman, so when I opened my waiting room door, I was surprised. A colorful scene greeted me. Elinor was a stylish thirty-something woman with long dark hair and bright pink lipstick. She was dressed in tasteful blues—navy leggings and a pale fleece sweatshirt with matching bulky sox—yet like so many women who hope to divert attention from their bodies by keeping the focus above their necks, she wore an oversized sweatshirt.

"Hi there, I'm Elinor," she said in a bubbly voice, and followed me into my office. Her long silver earrings swung gracefully as she spoke. "I'm 32, and this is my last attempt at fixing whatever it is that is wrong with me. I hope I'm not 'incurable.'" The last word weighed heavily in the room.

"Incurable is a strong word. How might you be incurable?"

She shrugged her shoulders and looked me directly in the eyes. "I lose it with food, you know. This is a fact. It's why I'm here. Except for food, my life is fine, but my bingeing is a nightmare. Something in me is off and makes me lose control when it comes eating. It's like there's an evil monster with a mind of its own that lives right here at my core." She gave her stomach a hearty slap.

"What can you tell me about the evil monster?"

"It's like a hurricane that sweeps through me. It knocks me out. Do you know what I mean?"

" I'm not sure I do, yet," I said, "but I'm curious. What else can you tell me?"

"You know how hurricanes can suddenly develop? How they unexpectedly can swirl up out of nowhere and hit with an incredible force? That's what I mean." Again, she slapped her belly.

"You mean, your binges hit you the way hurricanes hit—unpredictably and with a unbelievable force?" I said, wanting her to feel my listening presence.

"Exactly," said Elinor, appearing to be somewhat relieved. "Whenever I'm around food, I'm a wreck because I never know for sure when I'll be demolished." She paused. "That's exactly what it feels like—being hit by a binge is like being demolished or destroyed. When the hurricane hits, I'm lost. It doesn't happen *all* the time," she said, "not every day. But recently, my eating rampages are more frequent."

"Could you describe a 'rampage'?" She looked blank. "When was the last one?" She couldn't remember. Always curious about what pushes someone to seek help, I asked her, "What brings you here, now?"

"This probably sounds stupid, but I'm here because of a dress I bought two months ago. It's a beautiful silk, but I've never worn it and probably never will. I'll never fit into it. Now," she said, lowering her voice to a whisper, "I can't squeeze this gross monstrosity into anything at all." I leaned forward to hear her better. "I really make myself sick. I bet you never heard anything so stupid—coming to a therapist because a dress doesn't fit."

Elinor was not alone. She reminded me of countless women of all ages, shapes, and sizes who have been driven to my office by a tight pair of pants, a disastrous shopping expedition for a bathing suit, or a friend's unkind remark. When a person says, "I hate myself because I'm fat," I always wonder what intolerable feelings lurk beneath those words.

" I'm the heaviest I've ever been," Elinor went on. "I've gained 20 pounds since July. Twenty pounds in six months—can you imagine that? You're probably thinking, 'She's exaggerating.' But I'm not. I'm almost 150 pounds. At 5'6", that's sickening. Don't act surprised and say you never would have guessed—or some other stupid thing, like, 'You carry it so well!' You just can't see my bulges because I hide them underneath this baggy sweatshirt. Do you know I haven't worn a shirt tucked into a pair of pants in months?"

She calmed down and sighed, "But that's not the point. The point is, I'm not like some people who probably come in here and tell you they don't know why they're so fat." She knew *tons* of people who deceived themselves about their weight gain, but she was different. She knew quite well where the source of her misery lay. "I *could* be thinner. I'm overweight because I binge. It's as simple as that." And with the word "binge," her eyes filled with tears that she quickly brushed aside.

"My sister has been telling me for years that my eating problem is wrapped up with my mother. My sister is a therapist, too. She says we had a really rotten childhood and I should work on it." She paused. "But all therapists think that, don't they?"

"All therapists think what?"

"You're stalling," she said. "My sister has explained to me that whenever she doesn't know how to answer a question, she simply flips it back to the patient." Elinor beamed, looking like the cat that ate the canary. Was she being defiant or testing me? I wondered where to go next. Stay present with what is happening now, I reminded myself. "You're still stalling," she said. An uneasy silence grew.

"You might think I'm stalling," I finally said, "but I see it a bit differently. I do turn the focus back on you, that's true. That's because our job here is to understand you—your thoughts and feelings."

"You're avoiding my question: Do all therapists think that the source of all misery is a rotten childhood?"

"Do all therapists think misery is always about having a rotten childhood?" Repeating her words, I assumed she would think I was stalling again, but, in reality, I was mulling over this genuinely unanswerable question and her reasons for asking it. "I don't really know what all therapists think," I said. "Nor do I know the source of all misery. But you ask good questions and, really, I wish I had more answers." I wanted her to know that I was taking her seriously. "What I'm really interested in is you—and *your* misery."

Apparently satisfied, Elinor continued, "My sister thinks I'm an emotional eater. But that's my sister. She thinks everything is emotional. Like I said, she thinks our childhood was a mess and the fact that I don't remember a lot about it is only further confirmation. She says I've probably screened out the bad memories."

"What do you think about that idea?" I asked.

"I don't remember much, it's true, but is that so unusual?" Without waiting for my answer, she added, "But I'm not here to talk about my childhood, no matter what my sister thinks."

I was puzzled. Was she interested in exploring her past even though she was protesting? Or was she warning me to stay away? As Elinor's sister had pointed out, the fact that she didn't remember much probably meant that she had blocked a lot out. Unfortunately, though, people who protect themselves from knowing the past are doomed to repeat it. "Well," I said, "we're here to talk about your agenda, not your sister's or anybody else's."

Elinor remained quiet. When she finally spoke, her voice trembled. "I've got to lose weight. That's why I came."

"Tell me more," I said.

"My binges began to get worse three years ago, right after Meri was born." With the mention of her daughter's name, her face lit up.

"Tell me about Meri," I said.

"She's my life, " said Elinor, smiling, "I'm not kidding." She hadn't been prepared for how much she would love being a mother. "From the very first moment the nurse placed her in my arms, I was hooked, hopelessly in love. Her tiny toes and fingers were so perfect! We nicknamed her Meri, because from the first moment, that's what she's brought us—instant joy."

Elinor had intended to return to work when her baby was three months old, but that plan went out the window as soon as Meri was born. Even now, three years later, returning to the high-powered, fast-paced advertising job that had been her second home before Meri's birth held little appeal. Being a mother had transformed her life. In fact, getting pregnant again was already on her mind. "But I don't need to talk to you about Meri," she said. "My problems are food and my weight. I want to lose some weight before I get pregnant again."

The unadulterated adoration she expressed for Meri impressed me at first. Soon, however, her effusiveness began to ring my alarm bells. From experience, I knew that mothering is incredibly hard work, fraught with demands, and I was surprised to hear not a negative word. I wondered whether Elinor was ashamed to give voice to what I suspected were moments of confusion, frustration, and resentment—all normal feelings that are part of the mix of parenting. Many people try to be "perfect" parents in an attempt to repair the losses they endured in their own childhood. Was she burdened by some impossible, self-imposed definition of good mothering? Or, had becoming a parent stimulated memories from which she was trying to distract herself by bingeing? The more she told me about her daughter, the more I wondered, until finally, she repeated, "I don't need to discuss Meri. I want to lose weight and the question is, how? I know I'm overweight because I overeat. What I don't know is *why* I overeat."

I took another look at Elinor, this time scrutinizing her more carefully. To my eyes, she was an attractive woman—not a toothpick, but not particularly large, either. And this was not the issue, anyway. Elinor, like so many women, was not struggling with her body size but with her body *image*.

I was in a bind. I certainly didn't want to give her the impression that I agreed with her about her weight. And yet, if I were to tell her that she appeared to be of normal weight for her height, I might alienate her, for she was invested in her definition of her problem: She was fat. That's what had driven her to my office, and that's where I had to begin. I hoped that talking about her weight would eventually bring us in touch with her deeper issues, even if, initially, it might distract us from them.

"What else can you tell me about your eating?" I ventured.

"A lot," she said. "The only reason I don't weigh more than I do is that after I binge, I exercise religiously. And I am very careful about what I eat for a few days. Thank God I no longer have that anguish—those crazy crash diets always made things worse."

"Tell me about your anguish," I said, hoping that she'd pick up my emphasis on feelings, but she stayed on her track. What followed instead was her history of suffering as a failed dieter. She had tried them all: Scarsdale, Weight Watchers, 12-step, low-fat, no-fat, low- and high-carbohydrate, and her most recent failure, the Zone diet. She had begun "weight-watching" 22 years earlier when, at age 10, her mother put her on a cottage cheese diet in preparation for her sister's graduation party. Although she had a cloudy picture of her childhood, the agonizing details of that diet remained firmly etched in her memory: six weeks of tasteless cottage cheese (the small-curd kind) with canned peaches packed in water.

"Have you ever eaten those disgusting peaches?" she asked me.

"Incredibly, I have," I told her. In my mind, I recalled how badly I had felt as a sixth-grader, eating those same sickening peaches so I could fit into my pink organza graduation dress. Of course, I learned the lesson all dieters learn: Pounds lost on crash diets are quickly regained, plus more.

Elinor was the younger of two daughters. Her father, Ralph, was a compulsive eater and obese. Her mother, Bettina, who was an overweight child, had become a thin and glamorous woman. Throughout Elinor's childhood, her mother was admired for two things. First, she had lost weight and kept it off, which, according to Bettina, was no small feat! She was a living example of the notion that if you work hard enough, you can transform your life by transforming your body. Second, she was a fanatical cleaner. Every afternoon and much of the night, she scrubbed, polished, and sanitized their house. She slept late enough each day to get her "beauty sleep" (a high priority) and would arise just in time to meet Elinor at the school bus at 3 P.M., still in her bathrobe. The afternoon routine would unfold predictably. While Bettina busied herself "putting on her face" and then compulsively cleaning, Elinor busied herself with milk and cookies. And more cookies.

"It was so embarrassing when the other kids saw my mother in her bathrobe," Elinor said.

I was sure that she must have felt more than embarrassed, but for now, I asked, "Did your mother know how you felt?" Elinor, it appears, didn't tell her mother anything, and, instead, stuffed herself at the kitchen table. Thus began our journey of exploring her lifetime habit of overeating.

Joanna, Elinor's sister, was three years older. She resembled their mother; both were blond, petite, and pretty. Elinor was dark and pretty, but not petite. Like her father, she had a big frame, and when she reached puberty early, her "troubles" really started. She began sixth grade 10 pounds heavier than she had been at the end of fifth. Often, weight gained at the onset of puberty is naturally lost later on, but

Elinor's mother was not prepared to wait and see. Frantic that her daughter would be overweight, she scoured the neighborhood for the "best" of the diet doctors, reassuring Elinor, "You probably can't help it—you take after your Dad and his family, honey."

These words fell on Elinor's heart like a death sentence. She did feel more like her father than her mother, both temperamentally and physically, and for as long as she could remember, he had been the target of Bettina's and Joanna's scorn. "Gobble, gobble, gobble," Joanna would sometimes say when their father joined them at the dinner table, and Bettina would do nothing to stop her. Was that why Dad rarely came home until after she and her sister were in bed, Elinor wondered?

"Better now than later" was Bettina's motto regarding exercising, diet pills, and diet doctors. Boys simply don't like fat girls, she claimed. That's why she herself still continued to work so hard at looking good. Looking good mattered.

Growing up "big" had been a nightmare for Elinor, especially when it came to shopping. Several sessions later, as she began to connect the dots of her childhood, she would remember a particularly painful incident that had occurred the week before her thirteenth birthday. She and her mother were on a shopping expedition when they were joined by Aunt Esther and her three-year-old daughter, Dolly. With long blond hair, huge brown eyes, and pixie face, Dolly was an attention-grabber *par excellence.*

At one point, Bettina and Esther were trying on clothes in the dressing room of a chic boutique, and Elinor was left in charge of Dolly. The little girl was doing cartwheels in the aisle while an elderly couple looked on admiringly. Turning to Elinor, the man said, "What an adorable daughter. You're doing a great job with her!"

"I nearly died," Elinor said. She had assumed that she was mistaken for Dolly's mother because she was so fat. "I never told my mother what happened. I was too ashamed," she recalled sadly, with a faraway look in her eyes.

Our initial session was drawing to a close, when Elinor added, "By the way, I'm a victim of several failed therapies—a few with well-known experts." She had been seen sporadically by psychologists, social workers, and even a psychiatrist or two over the previous decade. Later on, it became clear that the phrase "been seen by" was a euphemism for superficial dabbling. She had never stayed with any one therapist for more than half a dozen sessions. She had grave reservations that therapy would ever help, but she was willing to give it one more try. She looked me in the eye. "Do you think I can be helped?" she asked. "Can you offer me hope?"

"Although I barely know you, yes, I believe healing is always a possibility. Each of us heals in a different way. Finding the right path can be a challenge, but yes, I feel hopeful for you. I couldn't do this work if I didn't." I thought I saw a sense of relief cross her face. "I'll tell you something else," I said. "You sound like a wounded veteran." She liked that phrase. If she was wounded rather than incurable, perhaps she might heal.

Since eating disorders never occur in a vacuum, I wondered how the rest of Elinor's life was going. "What about your husband, Jeff? You've barely mentioned him," I said.

"What about him?" she asked.

"I just wondered how you two are doing."

"He doesn't even know I'm coming here, and I don't want him to, either," she said. "Besides, this has nothing to do with him."

Perhaps this is enough for the beginning, I thought.

One week later, Elinor returned for our next session in a panic. "I should have asked you last time—what am I going to do about food? How do I know what to eat so I can avoid bingeing?"

Rather than focus on food and ask her to change what she was eating, usually a formula for failure, I decided to introduce her to the concept of "mindful eating." Basically, mindfulness means staying in the present moment and paying attention to what *is*, rather than letting yourself wander off into thoughts of what could be, should be, has been, or will be. We've all had times when we eat not because we're hungry, but simply to feel better when we're lonely, tired, angry, sad, or bored. Sometimes we eat to take our minds off what we're thinking or feeling. Mindful eating is based on a simple principle: Pay attention to your hungers.

"Just notice what's going on inside you," I told Elinor. "Taking the time to think about whether you're hungry and what it is you're hungry for is the first step in eating mindfully and healing your problem with food. Start by noticing feelings of emptiness and fullness. Paying attention in this way will help you tune in to your other hungers—for love, excitement, self-fulfillment, human touch, and so on. Eventually, you can learn what it is you need to live a more nourishing life and how you can feed your needs in other ways than eating."

I gave Elinor a few questions to think about: Am I hungry? What am I hungry for? How do I feed my heart? How do I feed my soul?

"I particularly liked your first two questions," Elinor said, opening the next session. She had nicknamed them "Judy's Mindful Eating Questions." They helped her to calm down and think before she acted—or ate—impulsively. They also made her aware of her eating patterns. The most startling revelation was that she often ate even though she wasn't a bit hungry. Another was that if she ate when she wasn't hungry, she binged, although she still had no idea why. All she could say was that a "dark hurricane" lived within her and could take over at any time.

"It's the eye of the hurricane that scares me," she said, describing her terror of the powerful hunger that unpredictably whirled through her. "It's the strongest at the eye." As she spoke, I recalled a television special I had watched the previous summer about hurricanes. Before the next session, I did a bit of homework.

"You know," I said the next time I saw her, "I was thinking about your fear of the eye of the hurricane. When you spoke about the eye, something didn't sit right." She looked at me with a puzzled expression. "The eye of the hurricane is not really a place of uncontrollable force. In fact, it's the opposite," I continued, explaining that the "eye" at the center of every hurricane is actually a very calm place. "Perhaps that's what you need—a calm place where you can go and be safe when the hurricane comes along."

She agreed. "That's exactly what I need to find—a place of inner calm. But that's really hard for me to do."

"Maybe we can create an imaginary 'eye,'" I said. "A place of safety where you can ride out the hurricane when it sweeps through you." Elinor was dubious. "Your imagination is the key here," I went on. After describing how imagery is useful in creating a safe place within, I led her into a relaxed state. We began by focusing on her breathing. Next, I gave her specific instructions for relaxing all the muscles in her body. Then I said, "See if you can remember, or revisit, a place that offers you a sense of safety and calm. You may need to go back many years, or you may recall a recent time, as recent as yesterday or even today." I paused to give her time to search within. "When you have such a place in mind, just nod your head."

Within a moment Elinor nodded. "Stay there and get a good feeling of what it is like to be in your safe place. Become familiar with this place where you can ride out whatever waves, troubles, or storms hit." Then I asked her to tell me about the place she had found.

With her eyes closed, Elinor said, "I see a big, brown leather chair. It's in my den. I love to curl up in this chair and think, dream, read…I can do whatever I want or need to do there."

"Know that you can return to this place in your imagination whenever the urge to binge hits," I said. "It's always available to you." I suggested that she spend a few minutes each day practicing the technique, and over the weeks, Elinor learned to apply it whenever the hurricane threatened to sweep through her. She binged less frequently, and, although she still didn't know where her compulsion to eat came from, she seemed increasingly curious about its possible roots in the past.

So, when Elinor whirled into my office in a state of agitated despair and said, "Perhaps this should be our last session," I felt as if the ground was disappearing under me.

What had gone wrong? What had I overlooked? Perhaps I had moved too rapidly. Or maybe we had gone too slowly. Should I have included her husband, who may have learned that she was in therapy and been hurt that he hadn't been included? My little bell within sounded again, reminding me that I didn't have to blame her or myself. Perhaps, if I, too, could stay centered and mindful, something new might emerge. So, I listened as Elinor talked.

Although she had been feeling better these past months, her recent playgroup binge was proof of what she had known all along: These good feelings couldn't last. The hurricane had hit her only hours before our session. She wasn't sure why it had returned or why she hadn't been able to control it.

"I just couldn't help myself," she said, as she wiped fresh tears from her eyes and related the story of her most recent "failure."

Elinor had joined a neighborhood mothers' group shortly after Meri's birth. Now, two years later, the newborns were toddlers and the group had expanded. Often it was a relaxing experience, but on this particular day, the children were unmanageable. Could I imagine how wild seven squabbling two- and three-year olds could be? I nodded. Yes, I could.

Melissa had started the day by throwing a block at Jayson, who never stopped whimpering. Justin refused to share his toys and was on a hitting jag. Randi was whiny and clingy. Temper tantrums, hitting, spitting—the atmosphere was frenzied. As Elinor described the pandemonium, I recalled how I had felt in those moments when my children were young: desperate, helpless, yearning to escape, and then guilty for feeling that way.

In an effort to restore peace, Helen, the hostess, suggested an early lunch. The presence of their lunch boxes had an immediate soothing effect on the children, but for Elinor, it was the beginning of a downward spiral. Although she wasn't particularly hungry, she decided to eat anyway, just to be sociable. She began with the cut-up vegetables she had brought with her, and within moments, felt ravenously hungry.

Was the hunger in her stomach or her heart? I asked. Elinor didn't know. She'd forgotten to check in with herself and had been unable to stay in the present. "Where were you?" I said. All she knew was that she had been nibbling on the carrots and celery when, suddenly, she found herself eyeing the cookies. "I found myself on automatic," she said. "Everything I've learned about mindful eating was gone, and I was in the food, reaching and grabbing." As fast as she could, she stuffed her mouth with cookies, potato chips, and Cheetos, which she didn't even like.

"Reaching and grabbing, just like a pig!" she said. When she repeated this phrase for the third time, my ears perked up. Her voice was different. I felt as if a harsh presence had sneaked into the room. "Why am I so upset? What is it with me?" she sneered contemptuously. I had a different question. I wondered what earlier agony had been triggered and whose critical voice was speaking inside her head.

Then I noticed that during this description, she was vigorously thrusting her arm forward, and opening and closing her fist with an energetic motion, particularly as she said the words, "reaching and grabbing." I sensed that she was struggling with an important experience that she couldn't express. "This image of you reaching and grabbing. I want to understand something more about what happened to you when you were sitting at the table in your playgroup. You felt out of control, reaching and grabbing, right?" She nodded.

"This reaching and grabbing—do you notice? It's here with us now. While you're describing what happened to you there, you're doing it here, with me." Following my gaze, she looked at her arm, which was suspended tensely in the air. And then I noticed that mine, too, was outstretched. In my desire to join in and understand her experience, unconsciously I had begun imitating her motion.

"Can we stay with it for a moment?" I asked. Elinor nodded. Silently we sat together, reaching and grabbing in sync. In the quiet, I felt the muscles in my hand and fingers tense and relax, and my connection to Elinor strengthen. Something in the room felt different, as if, by getting in touch not only with Elinor's feelings, but also with the body that she hated, we were discovering something new and significant.

"This is just what I was doing," she said. "I was reaching across the table, eating everything in sight and…"

"Elinor," I interrupted her, "I want to ask you to join me in an experiment. Let's stop talking for a few minutes."

"Stop talking?" she said, looking confused. "Why? Isn't the point of therapy to put your feelings into words?"

I explained to her that while talking usually does help us open up to our emotions, it can have the opposite effect and distract us from them. If we're quiet and listen to our bodies, we can sometimes reach a deeper place, because our gestures contain the imprints of our pasts. "If we can tap into our physical sensations," I said, "we give ourselves the chance to unlock and access old pain, and let go of it."

"Sometimes we must take risks in order to grow," I continued. "I think your body knows something about how you're feeling. Maybe if we sit quietly and focus on your what your body wisdom is saying, something new will emerge to help us understand you. Okay?" She nodded. "Let's just sit with this reaching and grabbing motion, and if your body knows something about you, it may tug you to a new place." So together we sat, silently reaching and grabbing and, as our breathing slowed, a calmness seeped into me. Soon, Elinor began to speak.

"I see myself as a little girl," she said. "I'm only a few years older than Meri. I'm standing on the counter in the kitchen, in the house that I grew up in where my parents still live. It's dark, early in the morning, and I'm reaching up into the cabinet to find something to eat." With these words, Elinor began to recall early memories of searching desperately for cookies on the highest shelf of the kitchen cabinet, while her mother lay sleeping.

"Stay with this image of you standing on the kitchen counter," I said.

"I keep sneaking a look at the door, afraid that my mother is coming in and will be furious with me."

"Stay there with little Elinor," I said, as she stretched back into a long-forgotten memory of hungrily reaching into the shelf where forbidden Oreos had been placed out of the reach of the chubby daughter.

"I see myself stuffing and cramming them into my mouth, trying to fill myself up fast before my mother wakes up and finds me." Did Elinor realize what an important discovery she had just made? I had suspected all along that emotional issues buried in Elinor's past were reenacted when she binged. Now, she was beginning to make this connection, too.

"Taste the cookies sliding into your mouth, the rich, creamy filling and chocolate patties," I said. Elinor opened her eyes and looked at me.

"I don't think I ever tasted them. I was eating too fast," she said mournfully as she made contact with the little girl standing on tiptoes on the kitchen counter, too ashamed of what she was doing to enjoy her secret feasts.

"What did you need as a little girl?" I asked.

"I needed my mother," she whispered. Pressing her hands against her forehead, she looked as though she was trying to ease an excruciating pain.

"Where was your mother?" I asked.

"She was sleeping."

"Do you have any idea why you didn't call her?"

In a sad, childlike voice, Elinor said, "Because she wouldn't have come. I couldn't make her wake up."

Although buried memories can trigger automatic behaviors such as bingeing, simply recalling the past does not necessarily heal a person. Revisiting emotional pain can actually re-wound rather than repair the soul, and the wounds themselves can become the core of one's identity. We all know people who endlessly recite the details of old injuries. However, while being absorbed in the pain of the past can inhibit renewal, remembering pain in the presence of a caring, supportive person is the bedrock of healing.

Elinor's retrieval of her memory was the beginning of a new phase of growth. By encouraging her to stay present to the pain of her past, I helped validate her childhood need for care and connection. She was amazed that simply talking about the past helped her feel better.

Over time, she became increasingly self-aware and understood how the self-defeating beliefs that she had developed in childhood still colored her life.

The first belief was, *I am fat.* The second was, *Fat people are disgusting.* This led to *I am disgusting* and *I'm not deserving of love.* Because her parents were not available to her when she needed them, she believed that she was not entitled to have her needs met. As she got older, this assumption coalesced and hardened her. She stopped asking or expecting others to be there for her. Rather than experience her hungers or rage about being neglected, she turned her aggression and disappointment on herself. Her belief, *I am not deserving of love*, was transformed into a more subtle message: "I don't deserve to be emotionally nourished."

This had dire consequences. While she may not have felt deserving, her hunger for contact and care remained. In numerous sessions, we came to understand how, as a child, she protected herself from experiencing her intolerable feelings of powerlessness and shame by turning to food when she couldn't wake her mother.

In the months that followed, more memories emerged. Elinor often felt that she was on an emotional roller coaster. She was deeply disturbed to think that parts of her past had been lost for years. Even now that they were accessible, she resisted accepting their significance. "What's the point of dredging up the past?" she would ask.

But one day, delving into her past yielded another important clue. She remembered that when she began bingeing on that ill-fated day at Helen's, she had felt helpless and out of control. Elinor finally began to see the connection between her bingeing and her feelings. Her binge had occurred when she felt powerless to reign in her daughter—as powerless as she had once been to wake her mother. Sadly, she realized that even now, she was automatically reenacting the strategy she had learned so well as a child. Rather than feel and talk about her painful emotions, she ate.

Elinor hated thinking of herself as having been neglected. But now, rather than relive the past and eat, she challenged herself to grapple with her emotions. "Talking with you not only helps me feel my feelings, but it helps me endure what I feel, too," she said.

Soon she became involved in soul-searching talks with her sister and eventually she approached her mother and father. A series of family sessions followed that helped her to further answer the question she had raised in our very first session: Is the present related to the past? The two were more intertwined than she had thought.

In the first meeting with her parents, Elinor began by expressing her anger and frustration. "Didn't you know that dragging me from diet doctor to diet doctor, beginning at age 10, would make me feel fat and hideous? Didn't you know how your emphasis on being pretty and thin was damaging to me?" She was surprised at how easy it was to put her feelings into words. But even more amazing were her parents' responses. Bettina confided a part of her own history that she had never shared. As a daughter of an explosive, alcoholic father, she had grown up with a constant fear of violence.

"Being pretty was my passport out of my father's house!" she said. She had learned to ignore her fears and feelings, first by perfecting her body, and later her home. Always, the focus on the outside distracted her from what was going on inside.

At another session, Bettina tearfully apologized and begged Elinor's forgiveness. "I encouraged you to be thin because I wanted you to be accepted and find love. I felt I had so little to offer you—but one thing I did know was being thin helped me attract your father." Although this explanation did not change the past, by listening to her daughter's pain, Bettina affirmed Elinor's reality. In apologizing for her own behavior, she revealed an empathic side that Elinor had never known.

Another part of Bettina's story emerged. After her daughters had left home, getting out of bed became more difficult. Her exhaustion had eventually forced her to seek psychological counseling. "In therapy I learned that cleaning was a way I hid from my feelings," she said sadly. "And the sleeping late—it wasn't just tiredness or beauty rest. I couldn't face my life. I couldn't face the fact that I was depressed." The unresolved fears from her childhood had bred a shameful silence that had lifetime consequences not only for herself, but for her daughters as well.

The family sessions offered Elinor the opportunity to heal with her father, too. Having been overweight his whole life had scarred him. Wanting to protect his daughter from his fate, he had unwisely supported Bettina's decision to put Elinor on a diet. "I never knew how harmful that was," he admitted.

And in the stories of his childhood, another piece of family history came to light. In an effort to spare his family from suffering the economic deprivation that had marked his childhood, he had worked two jobs, which created another problem—he was rarely home. Trying to be a devoted husband and father, he had been overworked, exhausted, and unavailable to Elinor. These sessions offered an opportunity for her to develop compassion for both parents and rebuild her relationships with them on a more authentic basis.

Some moments in therapy are turning points, and for Elinor, retrieving the memory of standing on the kitchen counter was one. Throughout the remainder of our work we revisited this image as I tried to help her come to terms with the sense of powerlessness that her sleeping mother had aroused in her. One day we tried the following guided imagery: We stood in the doorway of Bettina's bedroom, where, as a child, Elinor had stood so often, wishing her mother would wake up.

"What is your mom doing?" I asked.

"Sleeping."

"Can you see yourself asking your Mom to get up? To come into the kitchen?"

Elinor had closed her eyes. In a small voice, she said, "Can you get up, Mom?"

"What's happening?"

"She doesn't hear me," said Elinor, sadly.

"See what happens if you speak a little louder."

Speaking louder, Elinor said, "Get up, Mom!"

"What's happening now?" I asked.

Elinor shook her head. "Nothing."

"How do you look, standing at the door?"

"I am so sad. I look like I'm giving up. I'm thinking about going back to the kitchen—to the cookies."

"What do you need?"

In a stronger voice, Elinor said, "I need her to get up."

Realizing that Elinor could use my support, I asked her, "What will happen if you tell your Mom, as loudly as you can, that you need her?"

Elinor shook her head. "I can't talk any louder." She spoke in the voice of a small child.

"Do you need my help?" I asked.

"Yes."

"Is it okay for me to try to talk to your Mom?" Elinor nodded. "Okay, I'll give it a try." I told her to imagine Bettina sleeping on the couch in my office. Turning to the imaginary Bettina, I spoke in a loud, firm voice, "Get up, Bettina! Get up! Your daughter needs you! Are you listening?" At this point I turned back to Elinor and said, "How is your mother responding to me?"

"She's ignoring you," said Elinor. "Even for you—she won't get up!"

This experience offered Elinor a curative image by reminding her that no one, not even her therapist, could have budged her mother. It helped her realize that her feelings of powerlessness and ineffectiveness had legitimate roots. During this phase of therapy, we focused on helping her accept what had been, forgive herself for the solutions she developed as a child, and grieve for what she had missed.

A month later, Elinor waltzed into my office. "I'm feeling really good," she said proudly. "This weekend I managed to avoid what could have been a big binge!"

Elinor and Jeff had invited the whole family over for her sister's birthday. After all the guests had left, she was in the kitchen, cleaning up. "Suddenly I was nibbling on the leftovers. First pasta, then salad. When I got to the chocolate cake, I began getting that hurricane feeling. I had no idea why. Suddenly, I realized I wasn't the slightest bit hungry and I said to myself, 'Come on, Elinor, what's going on?'

"You'll never believe what happened—I remembered our conversation about the eye of the hurricane and I reminded myself about my safe place. I closed my eyes and put myself in the leather chair. 'Just breathe,' I told myself. Then it hit me—I was feeling all alone in the kitchen with those dishes. I'd been abandoned. Jeff was lying on the couch relaxing, watching an old Humphrey Bogart film, while I was cleaning up. I started to feel mad, but a little voice in my head reminded me that I could ask for help—I didn't have to do the dishes alone and I didn't have to eat. So I asked him to help me.

"At first he blew me off, but I was on a roll. I wasn't going to slip into bingeing again. So I went into the den, turned off the television and told him that my feelings were hurt. Guess what? He said, 'Leave the mess in the kitchen. It can wait! Come lie down with me. Let's watch the end of the movie—and then I'll help.'

"Wait," she said. "The story isn't over. I did something else un-usual for me. You know me—I am still my mother's daughter, and I can't leave dishes in the sink for five minutes. Ordinarily I wouldn't be able to enjoy myself with the kitchen in such a mess. But this time, I thought, I don't *want* to do all those dishes myself. And he did offer— I should *let* him help me. So I lay down on the couch, we watched the end of the movie, and eventually cleaned up together. Jeff even washed the floor—the job I hate the most!" Elinor was glowing, and so was I.

"There's more," she said. The next day she had gone food shop-ping with Meri. Without planning to, she bought two boxes of Oreos. "When I unpacked the groceries and saw them, at first I was alarmed. But eventually I understood what had happened." She looked me straight in the eye. "I put them on the highest shelf of the kitchen cabinets. Every day, I've gone in there, looked at them, and reminded myself, 'I'm not that little girl anymore! I don't have to eat when I'm not hungry. I have other ways to care for myself.' What do you think of that?" she said. Without waiting for me to speak, she continued. "One more thing. I've saved the best for last. I'm going to try to get pregnant— and not worry about the weight!"

Only weeks after the birth of her second child, Ben, Elinor came into my office. No longer relying on food to mask her pain, she was more present to her emotional life. Meri was adjusting to the presence of the new baby and, even when she threw a predictable tantrum, Elinor was able to ride the waves. She had been working hard at being more direct with everyone in her life. Her husband was more helpful than he had been before, an unanticipated delight. To her surprise, Bettina continued to be apologetic about the past and seemed genuinely interested in forging a better relationship with her and the grandchildren.

For most of the session, Ben slept peacefully in her arms. Then, suddenly, he opened his eyes. Elinor and I stopped talking. We looked at him, looked at each other, and my breath caught in my throat. Perhaps I was recalling my early days of mothering, the joys and struggles. Perhaps I was proud that I had been helpful to her. Perhaps I was reminded of the miracle of life and was simply overwhelmed.

"What is it?" she asked.

I told her that seeing her with her baby moved me in an inexplicable way. She seemed stunned and, as we sat in silence, tears in my eyes were mirrored by tears in hers. Several weeks later she told me that in that moment, she felt peaceful, proud, and beautiful. "Me, too," I said, remembering how hopeless we both had felt when she had threatened to quit therapy.

Although not a Freudian, I am guided by Freud's basic rule. To every patient he gave the same instruction, "Say everything." This rule was based on the notion that making room for *all* of one's thoughts and feelings is the core of health. In actuality, however, saying "everything" is not an easy task for anyone, especially for people with eating disorders. Years of pushing away unacceptable thoughts and feelings with "fat talk" stunts the capacity to be connected to one's inner life.

A friend of mine recently told me that the Spanish word *esperar* means both "to hope" and "to wait." Every day in my office I learn that, given time, the human spirit has an incredible capacity to repair itself. That knowledge helped me sit mindfully with Elinor through the storms of her life while she found that the tools for healing were inside her all along.

~

5

A Puppy Dog's Tale

History, despite its wrenching pain, cannot be unlived,
And if faced with courage, need not be lived again.
—MAYA ANGELOU

I was surprised to get a call last July from a young man named Eric, who told me that he was home from college for the summer and wanted to make an appointment. He didn't say why he wanted to come in, but I had to wonder: Did he have an eating disorder? Most boys his age choose male therapists. As it turned out, what led him to me was a talk I had given to the faculty of a local high school in the wake of the shootings at Columbine High School. The talk was about boys and the pressures on them to be tough guys. But Eric didn't yet know that this was his story. In fact, at age 20, he didn't know much about himself at all.

Eric's mother, Emily Johnson, had picked me from the list the family doctor had given her after Eric was taken to the hospital, having fainted while running on the boardwalk. The doctor must have realized that something was up; we were in the middle of a July 4th heat wave, and Eric had been running for over two hours. Emily recognized my name on the list. She was a social worker at the high school where I'd spoken that May after Columbine.

Originally, I'd been asked to talk about girls and eating disorders, but when the news broke about the shootings, I couldn't ignore it. I knew that what had happened in that community could happen anywhere, and that these troubled boys' behavior was related to what was going on with girls all over the country. "Girls," I said in my talk, "deal with emotional pain by turning inward, taking it out on themselves and developing eating disorders; boys act out their pain by being tough and aggressive towards others." It turns out I was unaware of how complex boys really are.

A few days later, Eric walked into my office wearing bicycle shorts, his face red, T-shirt drenched in sweat and clinging to his slightly flabby body. "I don't know why Doctor Januski wanted me to see a therapist," he said in a tone that implied, *Hey, let's not waste each other's time.* "I just got overheated, running. Sunstroke, right? That's a medical thing."

"How much were you running?" I asked him.

"Not a lot."

"What's not a lot?"

"Ten miles. That's not much."

"Maybe, maybe not," I replied. Although running every day can be a perfectly healthy activity, the 10 miles made me instantly suspicious. Compulsive exercising is a type of purging—a coping mechanism that can help a person disconnect from his or her feelings. What matters is the *meaning* of the exercise. If Eric *was* pushing himself, I needed to find out why. And that, I told myself, was going to be an uphill struggle. I knew that most boys don't talk easily about their lives, especially to adults, and I didn't have much time to soften Eric's armor. I had learned during our initial phone conversation that he would be going back to school in a few weeks.

"I noticed the bicycle shorts," I said. " How far did you have to ride?"

"From Massapequa. Not far." I thought that was a long trip in the midday heat, when most people would choose to drive, and I said so. Eric tossed his head. "That's nothing. Yesterday I did twice that—in less than two hours."

"Wow!" I said. "Are you training for a race?"

"Not exactly. I just have my goals."

The mention of goals caused a blip on my mental radar screen. Exercising to prevent weight gain is the main diagnostic criteria for what's known as "exercise bulimia." But, in answer to my questions, Eric insisted that, although he had been a chubby boy, losing weight was *not* one of his goals; he just liked to stay in shape. He told me that he ran ever morning, biked in the afternoon, and lifted weights daily. His stamina was improving rapidly, and he felt great.

"So, how long have you been doing this?" I asked him. Enthusiastically, he told me that he had been working out ever since he started high school—but that he'd *really* been challenging himself since he came home from college for the summer.

"I like challenges," he said.

"It sounds like you've really been pushing yourself. What's it like, being home?"

"It's fine. It's good to have some time to myself after sharing a dorm apartment with two loud beer-drinkers."

"Getting away from all that must be good . . . and not so good," I said. "It must take some adjustment."

"Adjustment?"

"Well, for example, some kids say it's hard coming home from school and finding they don't have many of their old friends left." Eric looked stunned. Then embarrassed.

"Did you talk to my mother?" I told him that I hadn't, and asked him why he thought so. "Oh, nothing. It's just that—well, an old friend of mine died right before I came home, and she probably thinks I'm having a hard time over it. Is that why she told me to call you?"

"I have no idea," I told him. "But if you're asking me if you're here to help you deal with grief over a friend's death, that's for us to figure out."

"I'm dealing fine with it. It's really not a big deal. I mean, it's a terrible thing for his family and everything, but I'm okay. Paul and I didn't hang out that much since high school, anyway." And with that, he gave me a "Can I go now?" look, as if he'd been called to the principal's office and the ordeal was over.

"You know," I told Eric, "you're reminding me of when I was around your age and lost someone close to me. I spent a week shopping with my mother instead of thinking about how it felt to lose him." Eric looked annoyed.

"This is different," he said. "Paul was just a kid who lived next door and we used to be best friends, but now he's more like a family friend, you know? I mean, was. His mom and my mom are friends. I think my mother's taking it hard, and I can't imagine how Paul's parents are dealing with it. I make a point of walking the long way around the block just so I don't run into his mother, because seeing me would probably freak her out."

"It would be hard for her," I agreed, struck by how sensitive Eric was to everyone's pain but his own. "However, it might help her, too. Most people who lose someone they love want to share memories. And," I added, "maybe making contact would also help you."

"Whatever."

By the time our session was over, Eric had given me the bones of the story. His father had called him in the middle of finals week to tell him that Paul had been in a car crash and was in a coma. Things didn't look good. The next day, he called again with the news that Paul had passed away during the night. The funeral was to be held a few days later, before Eric would get home. Since then, he had learned no more about his friend's death or the funeral.

In fact, Paul's name never came up at home. Eric's father wasn't "much of a talker," and his mother was emotionally fragile when it came to loss. "She just can't deal with it," Eric told me. "Her brother died when she was 15, and . . ." He didn't want to upset her by asking about his friend, and she hadn't offered to talk about it. I wondered if Mrs. Johnson was as fragile as Eric believed her to be, or if she was simply being as protective of him as he was of her.

"It sounds as if Paul just disappeared off the face of the earth. Nobody's talking about him," I said. "I was thinking about how all of this coincides with you starting to exercise so hard. Do you think there might be a connection?" Eric looked at me as though I was speaking Greek.

"You seem surprised by the idea," I continued, "but losing someone can hit hard, even someone who's become a part of your past, like Paul. Nobody wants to suffer, so when bad things happen, sometimes we turn away from them instead of allowing ourselves to feel the pain. But the painful things live on inside us anyway. Even though you're not openly grieving Paul's death, you might still be grieving inside."

I wanted Eric to understand that his exercising could be an emotional release valve. Having suffered my own loss early in life, I know how easy it is to distract oneself from grief by staying busy. Sitting with pain, while emotionally difficult, is the only way to work through it. "Tragedy can pull us down or be an opportunity for growth," I told Eric at the end of our first session. He nodded, rose silently, and left.

My first goal was to help Eric connect to his grief and see the link between it and his exercising. So I was pleased when he returned the following week and told me that he had paid a visit to Paul's family. He'd been thinking about what I'd said about it helping Paul's mom.

"How was it?" I asked him.

"Probably a bad move," he replied. "She started crying and just couldn't stop. All she could do was hug me and cry. It was awful. I didn't know what to say."

"Well, her crying isn't a bad thing, and words aren't always the best comforter," I said. "Sometimes we just need to let the tears flow. Do you ever cry?"

"Me?"

"Yes. Do you ever *want* to cry?"

"Maybe I want to once in a while, but I'm not a little kid any more."

"Meaning only little kids cry?"

"Well, little kids and girls—women, you know. I mean, my mom cries sometimes, my little sister cries *a lot*."

"Have you ever seen your dad cry?"

Eric laughed, "You don't know my dad. He would never cry. He really deals with stuff, you know? Never lets it phase him."

I wasn't surprised to learn that Eric's father, like many men, held to traditional notions of "appropriate" maleness. He was a serious, hardworking man who had connected to his son through ball games and woodworking. On his desk, I later learned, he kept a framed photo of Eric from Little League. When Eric made noises about dropping softball during fourth grade, his father set aside weekends to give his son batting practice. Dad was Eric's model of what a "real" guy is, and Eric was eager to please him, even though he himself had never been "that hot" at team sports and was into different things, like photography and guitar.

As a young boy, in fact, he'd felt closer to his mother. A woman with artistic inclinations, she was good at "feelings talk," as Eric put it. "I hear her with her friends, and they can go on forever!"

As Eric talked, I formed a picture of a boy who had been pushing himself since adolescence to meet his father's expectations and fit in with the "right" guys. This picture came into clearer focus when I asked again about Paul. "Paul and I drifted apart some," Eric said, "but he always stuck by me. He was a good guy."

"Stuck by you?" I asked. It turned out that Paul had been loyal to Eric through a year in high school when Eric was having trouble with the school jocks, even though Paul had become a jock himself.

"Tell me more about that," I suggested, and for the rest of the session, we explored Eric's history as a boy among boys. Everything seemed smooth until he hit eighth grade, which was when he turned from a skinny kid into a slightly pudgy boy. "Before that, I could eat a box of donuts and it wouldn't make any difference, but suddenly I had, like, this belly, and one day I'll never forget, a kid called me 'fatso.' He was with a bunch of other guys and I was by myself, or I might have laid into him. Instead, I just walked away feeling like a total jerk."

I pieced together more of Eric's story. After he was teased in eighth grade, he turned to exercise. It was a pattern that I knew well from my work with eating-disordered girls. The problem often starts with weight gain at adolescence, which can make kids feel self-conscious and out of control, which then leads to exercise, dieting, or a combination of the two. Eric had joined his father's morning crunch routine. "Dad would breeze though his 20 crunches, and then he'd stop mid-crunch, hold it, and say, 'This is relaxing—how about you?' and I'd still be struggling to get to my fifth or sixth. If Mom came in she'd be furious and tell him to stop torturing me, but I didn't mind."

Over the next couple of sessions, Eric revealed details of having been bullied, teased, and belittled throughout his junior-high and high-school years. "It wasn't that big of a deal," he insisted as I probed, "although tenth grade could have been better."

"Tell me about tenth grade," I said, guessing that this was the year that Paul had "stuck by him." Initially, Eric was reluctant to talk about it. "I don't really remember too much," he said, but toward the end of a session he brought up an incident that was lodged in his memory. It was during a little league playoff game. Eric had been daydreaming in the outfield and missed two fly balls. When the coach took him out of the game and yelled at him on the bench, Eric almost started crying. Another kid noticed, and said in a voice loud enough for everybody in the dugout to hear: "Hey, faggot, did your mother forget to give you her hanky?" The next day, somebody had put a box of tissues on his homeroom desk, the first of many.

"It sounds like you were really tortured," I said.

"I dealt with it. Could have been worse. At least Paul stayed my friend. He'd see me sitting alone in the cafeteria and come sit with me." Eric looked down at the floor. "You know, I just thought of him and felt kind of sick. It happened the other morning, too. I woke up with a hole in my stomach. For a second I didn't know why it was there, and then I remembered."

"It's hard to lose someone," I said. "It's also hard to be rejected by your friends. In fact, a year of small jabs can be just as tough emotionally as a friend dying." We were both quiet for a few moments, each feeling the pain of our losses, the sores of our rejections. "Where are you now?" I asked Eric. He was still reliving his tenth-grade miseries.

"The worst thing is, I couldn't stand up for myself," he said. "Those guys were so powerful, they made me feel like a stupid little nerd. I guess I withdrew. I hung around the house, and my parents wouldn't leave me alone, always hounding me, 'What's up? Why don't you go out and have some fun?' I couldn't tell them what was going on. It would have made my mom sad. And Dad—well, he would have been disappointed. So I just stayed home, and the more I hung out by myself, the more I felt like a loser."

It's not unusual for kids to be shunned during adolescence, and the consequences can be devastating. While we tend to think of cliques as a "girl" phenomenon, boys experience shunning, too; in both cases, this can lead to low self-esteem, depression, and a tendency to see things in black or white. When they are young, kids look to their families for love, approval and a sense of themselves, but as they grow into the junior-high years, they develop a powerful need to belong. The world beyond home opens up, and peers count for more and more. The crowd becomes like a mirror. When friends aren't accepting, kids find themselves unacceptable; when rejection is levied, they blame themselves. Kids who are rejected are also angry. As I told the faculty members that day at the high school, some take it out on others, some take it out on themselves. And because their self-image at this age is still so fragile, the teases and taunts they experience can have a long-lasting effect on the way they see themselves, leaving them, even as adults, vulnerable to feeling rejected.

"Habits cover wounds," I told Eric. "What's important is that we're beginning to understand that what happened did, indeed, hurt you." Eric shifted awkwardly in his chair.

"I guess so," he said, and then he looked at me and asked, "How did you know? I mean, I thought you were wacky when you kept asking me about Paul and my other friends."

At that moment, I made a decision. "I'll tell you how I knew," I said. "Because I had an experience like yours when I was in my last year of junior high. Even now, when I look back, I remember eighth grade as a nightmare."

I told him about the most miserable year in my life, when the ringleader of a vicious group of girls in my Long Island town singled me out. "You'd have thought that at my age, I would have long forgotten," I went on. "Not so. I want to tell you a story about something that happened to me just a year ago that reminded me how wounds live on in unexpected ways."

I was at the theater with my husband, sitting in the balcony before the curtain rose, and I leaned down. There she was—my junior-high tormentor. Just seeing her face made my stomach drop. It was as if a forty-year-old wound had burst open. Suddenly, she looked up and waved. The house lights went down, the play started, and all I could do was remember that miserable year in school. I felt so many different ways—nervous, powerless, bitter and vengeful—all at the same time. I couldn't believe that those old emotions were still alive. "I guess that's how I understood your pain," I said, "because I know that these experiences stay with us."

Eric grinned. "You know, if I hadn't passed out on the boardwalk, I never would have been thinking about all this."

We had already discussed the fact that the next session would be our last. Although Eric was still exercising regularly, his workouts were shorter and less frequent. Our conversations had made him aware of his tendency to minimize emotional pain and he could now see that abusing exercise was a way to purge unpleasant feelings. Most importantly, he was curious about his inner life and more comfortable with "feelings stuff."

"So now," I said, "try to pay attention to your exercising. I'm not saying that exercise is bad. Everyone knows it's part of a healthy lifestyle, and it'll probably be a part of your life forever. That's fine, unless it's hiding something."

Eric arrived late for that final session. He flopped into his usual chair and looked around my office as if he was searching for a starting point. After what seemed like a long time, he said, "I saw a pretty funny movie yesterday."

"What was it?" I asked, wondering what Eric was really trying to talk about.

"*The Full Monty*. Have you seen it? It's about these six English guys who are out of work and decide to do a strip routine to earn money. It's hilarious." I hadn't seen it, but I'd heard about it from my son, who also had found it very funny.

"I know the story line," I said. "What do you think made you laugh?"

"I dunno. I guess because these guys were so . . . Well, they really didn't look like stripper material." Eric looked around again, awkwardly. "This one guy didn't want to go through with it because he was really ashamed of his body, and no matter how much he dieted, he couldn't lose weight. That was funny. I mean, that's a girl thing, right? Worrying about dieting and stuff."

"It's not just a girl thing," I replied. "I've met a lot of boys and men who feel just as uncomfortable about their bodies as girls do. The only difference is that they don't talk about it."

Eric didn't respond. I knew he was leading up to something, so I waited through several moments of silence until he blurted out, "Dr. Rabinor, I lied to you, or at least, I just haven't been 100 percent truthful." He paused to catch his breath. "There's something I didn't tell you. I vomit. I'm bulimic. I've never told anyone. I can't stand that it's the truth, but it is, and now I'm leaving for school next week, and I don't know what to do."

I wasn't surprised. It takes time for most patients to talk about the deeper things that trouble them. Often, facts trickle out slowly. But I felt badly for Eric. He was filled with shame about his bulimia. I heard it in his voice and saw it in his eyes. I guessed that he also felt badly about having withheld the truth from me, so I said, "I'm glad you've told me about this. It's a hard thing to admit to somebody else. We all protect ourselves by keeping silent."

Looking at his feet, Eric said, "I just couldn't bring myself to tell anyone, even when it was really bad." Instead, he searched out books and magazine articles, looking for clues and advice. "Everything I read about bulimia" he told me, "said it's a girl's problem. And that just made it worse."

"It might seem as if this is a girl's thing," I told him, "just as you might think that heart disease is a guy thing. The fact is, over the last couple of decades, more and more women have been suffering heart attacks and more and more men have been diagnosed with eating disorders. Both sexes are coming under the same types of pressures. Women have the stress of high-stakes jobs and men have to compete with idealized images of hard male bodies. You probably know from your reading that bulimia can be dangerous," I added. Eric nodded.

"That's why I'm glad I told you," he said with apparent relief.

I went on to say that while we hadn't worked on his bulimia, I felt sure that if he continued with a new therapist at school, he'd have a good chance of recovering. Not wanting him to lose momentum, I mentioned that most large campuses have mental health services that address eating disorders. Eric looked visibly distressed. That was not an option for him, he said. He did know a few girls who attended bulimia support groups on campus, but there was no way he was going to join one and be the only male! I reassured him again that bulimia was not *only* a female disorder, but I understood his concern, and added that before he left for school, I would try to find a therapist off-campus for him to see.

Eric spent the rest of that session filling me in on his bingeing and vomiting. He had been doing both, as well as losing himself in exercise, ever since that incident in high school when he was rejected. Sometimes the bulimia disappeared for several weeks, but it always came back when he felt particularly stressed about something, whether it was an impending midterm or a first date. I explained that eating disorder symptoms are a way of communicating, using the body rather than with words. I wanted him to go back to school with the awareness that the urge to overexercise or throw up was a signal that something else was bothering him that needed his attention. As we talked, we went over the triggers that led him to binge and vomit, which were the same emotional issues that drove him to run for miles: rejection and abandonment, both different faces of loss. This time, it was Paul's death; at other times, it was the sense that someone was pushing him away.

"I've noticed that sometimes, even if we don't really care about someone, the very fact that they reject us feels devastating," I said. "It's surprising how, even if we don't want the person as a friend, we want them to accept us."

"That's true," Eric agreed. "I guess I never thought about it that way. I mean, I can't stand it if I think someone doesn't like me, even a stranger. Why *is* it such a big deal, being accepted?"

"Why do you think?"

"I suppose it's because if someone rejects me, it's like they're saying I'm not good enough. But good enough for what? For whom? Maybe what they think doesn't matter if I don't even want to hang out with them."

"Maybe not," I replied. "But the important thing is knowing what you're feeling and being able to sit with it. That's sometimes hard to do, but we've been working on it."

Eric had drifted off. Looking perturbed, he told me that most of the articles he'd read about eating disorders said that they had roots in the family. "My parents are really good to me," he said. "They really didn't do anything. It's me who has this problem."

"Human development is mysterious," I replied. "What makes you *you*, or me *me*, is impossible to say for sure. But one thing we have learned is that hurtful experiences leave scars. Although your parents aren't perfect, and most aren't, what we are addressing here are things that had nothing to do with them."

Our session was ending. "I'll miss talking with you about all this stuff," Eric said somewhat awkwardly, and I realized how much had happened in our short time together.

"I wonder if you're aware of how much you've changed," I asked him. "You're able to think more deeply about your life. I think you realize now that what you're doing, whether it's exercising or vomiting, is a cry for help. And thank goodness, you're better at voicing your cries." Eric gave me an embarrassed grin. "But I'm curious," I went on. "Why were you finally able to tell me about your bulimia today?"

"Well, you remember last time?" he asked, "when you told me about the friend who tortured you in high school. All week I kept remembering little pieces of your story. I guess it just made me feel like I could tell you the truth."

Eric's words didn't really surprise me. I'd thought we had a solid connection, but all relationships are founded on trust, and building trust takes time and an occasional risk. I had risked doing what was frowned upon in my training: I had revealed myself. But in doing so, I let Eric know that I had walked his walk. I had seen, heard, understood, and embraced him in all of his complexity, and this had opened the door for him to reveal himself to me.

Before Eric left, I told him that he could use me as a bridge while he checked out the new therapist. I gave him my e-mail address as well as my phone number, and was mildly surprised not to hear from him for several weeks. When my colleague in Chicago called to thank me for the referral and spoke enthusiastically about their first session, I felt relieved.

A couple of days later, however, I did hear from Eric's mother, who called to thank me for helping her son. How was he progressing? Was there anything she should be doing? I explained that although I'd seen Eric only a few times, I thought he was doing a lot of good work on his own. I added that with college-aged kids who are motivated to be in therapy, I have found it best for parents to step back unless they are invited into sessions. "Give him a little time to get acquainted with the new therapist," I said, trying to be reassuring.

I finally heard from Eric a month and a half later, when I was downloading my e-mail one morning and found a message, dated two days earlier.

Hi Doctor R,

I bet you wonder what happened to me. Sorry I didn't write but getting back to school was really hard. I'll be home in a few weeks for Thanksgiving and wonder if I could come in to see you?

—Eric

PS- that other doctor? He didn't work out. We just didn't click.

I replied:

Dear Eric,

Glad to hear from you. Thanksgiving is six weeks away. If you'd like to set up a phone session, give me a call.

While phone therapy is never my treatment of choice, I've found it to be a practical way to stay connected with college students who are moving back and forth. In fact, some people seem to find that the distance actually helps them feel less self-conscious, making truth-telling easier. I'll always remember when a middle-aged woman with whom I was working opted for a phone session during a snowstorm and revealed that she'd been raped when she was 19. That session was the turning point in her treatment.

So, the week after I received Eric's e-mail, he and I had our first session of weekly phone therapy. I asked him why things hadn't worked out with the new therapist, and he said something about the doctor wearing a three-piece suit. Right away, I realized that my colleague must have seemed too traditional to Eric. My guess was that the suit was not the real problem, but his style of therapy. A momentary feeling of regret surged through me.

"How did he make you feel?" I asked Eric.

"Bad."

"What kind of bad?"

There was no answer for a moment, and then Eric's voice came back: "He was so quiet that I thought he didn't like me." I explained to Eric that therapists are trained to listen more than talk, and that he probably misinterpreted the doctor's silences as a type of rejection. Then we spoke again about how much Eric needed to be given signs of acceptance in order to feel comfortable.

"How did you feel when I didn't answer your e-mail right away?" I asked him, remembering that I hadn't checked my mail the day that Eric sent his message. Once again, there was no reply. "You know," I told him, "I was away for the weekend when your e-mail came and after I replied to you, I thought to myself, 'I bet he felt horrible when he didn't get a response.' Do you see why it's good for you to pay attention to how you feel, and when you notice that something makes you feel rejected, you need to check it out? There are always going to be times when people make you feel that way, whether they mean to or not. Learning how to identify and examine those feelings will help you get through life. It's something to work on, because I think you've been taught that boys are supposed to ignore their feelings, especially uncomfortable ones, rather than hold them up to the light."

I said that I had an exercise that might help, and suggested he imagine a container that could hold every disturbing feeling that came into his mind. He didn't have to know what each feeling was, only that he was experiencing some kind of discomfort. The container, I told him, had a special opening that would allow him to take out any of the feelings he put in there and work on them whenever he wanted. Only he would be able to open the container. Eric imagined a huge safe and saw his disturbing thoughts and feelings go into it. Several days later, he e-mailed me.

> Hi Dr. R,
>
> I wanted to tell you that the safe is filling up. I thought that exercise was a bit hokey when you told me about it, but a couple of times the last few days, things happened that made me feel bad, and I put my feelings in the safe. I didn't even think about them until I sat down to write this e-mail. What do you think of that?

During our next phone session, Eric told me about one of the events that had made him feel bad. He had learned that some fellows he knew were planning a hiking trip and hadn't included him. They eventually invited him two days later, but for those two days, he was miserable, "sweating bullets." Just before the invitation came, he remembered the exercise and put his feelings of being an outsider, unwanted and unwantable, in his safe.

I explained that getting our feelings into the container is the first part of the exercise; the next part is getting them out. "Reading our bad feelings, giving them names, makes them easier to handle and teaches us about ourselves and other people. Most boys never learn how to do this," I told him. "It's important, though, because uncomfortable experiences are part of our lives forever."

I suggested that he might enjoy a book I had recently read, *Tuesdays with Morrie* by Mitch Albom. It tells the story of a young man who spends several months paying weekly visits to his dying college professor, Morrie, a wise man who wants to share his life's lessons. One of the lessons is knowing your feelings. Morrie explains that when he learned he was dying, he allowed himself to fully experience all of his emotions—self-pity, anger, rage, fear. Knowing them allowed him to move on without letting them consume him.

The next time we talked, Eric sounded excited. "We're doing this gender unit in psych," he said. "We had an amazing class today. We really *are* all products of our environment. Not just that—the whole way we think about what it means to be male or female . . . I mean, who would I be if I'd been born male in a different culture? Or a different time? It makes me think about my dad."

"What have you been thinking?"

" I thought, maybe he'd like to be able to, you know, cry or even say he's miserable once in a while."

"One thing your dad hasn't had to worry about as much as you have," I said, "is the way he looks. You've grown up at a time when boys are under as much pressure to care about their physical appearance as girls.

The next day, I e-mailed Eric an article from the *The New York Times* about the increase of eating and body-image disorders in males. It pointed to the fact that boys tend to tease one another about the way they look as a way of shutting out their own feelings of self-consciousness. They're as worried about their bodies as girls, but can't talk about these anxieties because admitting to such things is tantamount to being "sensitive," which is like saying "girlish." Much of the time, boys don't even know that they're feeling ashamed or unsure of themselves, because they're so out of touch with their emotions. "It goes very, very deep, this culture of cruelty," I wrote.

Eric and I continued working together for the next six months, alternating between phone, e-mail, and live sessions, a kind of "patchwork-quilt therapy." In the spring, when his paternal grandmother died suddenly, Eric returned home for the funeral and week of *shiva*, the mourning period that followed. His Jewish family participated in many religious rituals, and Mr. Johnson stayed dry-eyed throughout. Eric understood him better now, and was surprised at the depth of his own emotions. "I didn't know Grandma Ida that well, but when I was at the cemetery, shoveling the dirt over her casket, I felt these tears welling up out of the blue. And then, this is the really weird thing, I got a memory of Rusty. He was my dog when I was small."

Rusty, a Collie, had died when Eric was seven. As many parents do in an effort to spare their children grief, Mrs. Johnson quickly replaced Rusty with another Collie, but Eric never really got attached to her.

"Your mother was doing what she thought was best for you," I explained. "Lots of parents make the mistake of trying to protect their kids from sadness by substituting something new for something lost—whether it's a toy or a pet—instead of helping them to learn that loving deeply involves hurting deeply. That's part of life. But you know, I remember my aunt telling me, at my father's funeral, 'Every loss brings up all our others.' It's true. Instead of mourning Rusty's death when you were seven, you're mourning it now—and Paul's. The loss of your grandmother is giving you that opportunity."

A few weeks later, Eric was back in school and missed one of our scheduled phone sessions. He left a message for me the next day to let me know that he had been at the hospital with a sprained ankle. I was worried. His injury would prevent him from exercising. Would he resort to vomiting instead? But, when we next spoke, he assured me that, although he had had a bulimic episode once when he came home from the emergency room, he was able to connect it to his fear of not being able to exercise. Having had this realization, he didn't binge and purge again. He was even able to accept gaining a little weight.

"I'm pretty busy with school work," he told me, "and I'm hanging out with this guy, Rick, who brought me to the hospital. He's putting together a band and I told him I play guitar, so we're working on some songs. I actually didn't go to a frat party last night because I wanted to practice with Rick. Can you imagine! I think I understand better which friends are good for me."

"Wonderful," I said. Small changes like the one that Eric had made are what heal us. Big insights are important and help us grow, but it's the little things we do to break old patterns that change our lives. And Eric continued to take small steps. In his next e-mail, he wrote:

> Hi Dr. R,
>
> My ankle's better. I'm running every morning with a couple of other guys, just six miles. I haven't done any of that other bulimic stuff since I sprained my ankle—although a couple of times I almost did. So far so good.
>
> PS-Things are going well here. In fact, I'm feeling pretty good about things in general. Rena is coming to see me at school this weekend. Wish me luck!

I was more than pleased. When Eric was home for his grandmother's funeral, he had reconnected with Rena, an old friend from high school. They had been on the phone every night. "We got along really well," Eric told me during our next phone session. "I feel so comfortable around her, sometimes it scares me, but she's really my type."

Eric seemed to be headed in a good direction. He was learning to accept himself for who he was—a young man who liked playing guitar more than softball. He seemed more appreciative of his strengths and less anxious about disappointing his father. At the same time, I knew that he was not 100 percent out of the woods. He was still vulnerable. Eating disorders often reoccur at moments of transition, and any transition, even one that is positive, can be stressful. How would he handle the normal ups and downs a relationship would inevitably bring? How would he weather graduating in just a few months?

A few weeks later, Eric cancelled our weekly phone session. He told me that as much as he enjoyed talking to me, he was just too busy right now with band practice. Rena had been coming to see him regularly and his life was jammed. We agreed to speak every other week, and eventually monthly. In May, he graduated and seemed to cross that hurdle without tripping. Shortly thereafter, he came home for a few weeks and came in to see me for a final goodbye. The next time I heard from him was in a postcard from Bolivia. "Rena and I are working for Habitat for Humanity this summer. What an amazing country! Thanks for everything."

Just recently, I was invited to another local high school to talk at an all-girls assembly. A sophomore had just died from anorexia, and the principal wanted me to do some prevention through consciousness-raising about gender stereotypes. I had given this kind of talk at several schools and often started with the nursery rhyme, "Sugar and spice and everything nice, that's what little girls are made of ... "

As I thought about what I was going to say, I realized that until I met Eric, I had ignored the other half of that rhyme: "Frogs and toads and puppy dogs' tails, that's what little boys are made of." I'd spent years empowering women to be in touch with who they are on the inside and not buy into cultural brain-draining messages like, "A pretty face is like an American Express card—it will take you anywhere." But now I knew the extent to which boys, too, are limited by cultural stereotypes like, "Big boys don't cry."

At the time that Eric told me he was bulimic, I had treated only a handful of males with eating disorders and didn't feel very knowledgeable; few of my colleagues had much experience, either. So I did what I always do when faced with a new challenge, and I scurried to the library. There I found little about boys and eating disorders, but in what I could find, the experts agreed that boys develop bulimia and anorexia for the same reasons as girls: low self-esteem, the need to be accepted, depression and anxiety, and feeling that their lives are out of control.

When Eric told me about his adolescence, I recalled a story my grown son told me recently about how freaked out he was when, in summer camp, some boys in his bunk set a mouse on fire. He didn't let his bunk mates know his feelings; he had to be "manly" and participate in this cruel act.

Males in our culture grow up with damaging messages that force them to be tough, to be ashamed of even experiencing a whole range of "soft" emotions; anger is one of the few permissible responses. But, while we've mobilized around the task of helping girls to find their voices, we've paid no attention to boys' silences—especially to those boys who, instead of acting out, quietly starve or purge themselves, or exercise to the point of exhaustion.

All of this went through my mind as I prepared for my upcoming assembly. Boys, too, need eating-disorder awareness and prevention. They need to hear how they're victims of role and body stereotypes, and a deeply divisive, competitive society that makes emotionally intimate connections so difficult. Boys are cheated, just like girls, which is what I told the high-school principal when I called to tell her that I wanted my talk to be for *all* of the kids in the school. I knew that most of the boys probably would snicker at my "feelings talk," but I figured that maybe one or two of them, like Eric, needed to hear me say that they were not alone, and that eating disorders are not just for girls.

6

The Air Was Thick with Promise

It is our light, not our darkness, that frightens us.
—NELSON MANDELA

We all love success stories. For me, it's an exhilarating feeling to say goodbye to a patient who enters therapy hurting and leaves because she is no longer in pain. But not every story ends so happily. When Julia left my office, my heart was heavy, for although she didn't show it, she was suffering. This beautiful human being was still trapped in a starving madness. I have never been in her particular prison, but I understood her pain, because I, too, have felt wounded. With help, I have healed, and perhaps my struggles with life's bumps have made me want to help others get better. But working with Julia taught me a few new lessons: to live with uncertainty and, especially, to accept my own limitations as a therapist. Through all the ups and downs of her treatment, she reminded me that when a person isn't ready to change, there is nothing I can do but patiently wait.

I hadn't heard from Julia for six months and had begun to accept that her "break" from therapy was permanent. Then I got an unexpected message from her on my answering machine. "We haven't spoken in a while, but you've been on my mind," she began. Now she had "something new" to discuss with me and wanted to set up an appointment.

Listening to the slow, lyrical cadence of her voice, my mind drifted back to the days when we would sit in my office, probing her troubled New Orleans upbringing. Within moments, the sadness of that memory was replaced by hope. Perhaps the relentless grip of her anorexia had loosened. Maybe she realized that she had left therapy prematurely. I found myself still wishing that she'd return. After all, it's not easy to let go of someone you care so much about. As I dialed her number, I realized that I was already back on the emotional roller coaster of optimism and pessimism that had marked our two-and-a-half-year relationship.

Julia's soft hello interrupted my thoughts. Yes, I did have an appointment available on Thursday, I told her. Yes, I too, was looking forward to our meeting.

"Can I tell you why I called?" she asked.

"Sure," I said, filled with anticipation.

"Do you remember my ridge?"

My elation evaporated. She had not called because she realized that her anorexia was still a problem, but because a plastic surgeon she'd consulted had insisted upon it. She wanted to have a "disgusting ridge," the result of a cesarean section, removed, and the surgeon required patients with a history of eating disorders to "check in" with their therapists. Many of these patients, he had told her, were dissatisfied with his work because what they wanted to fix wasn't fixable with surgery. I thought, How true: People with eating disorders hope to soothe what hurts on the inside by changing the outside.

Julia's call left me feeling confused. In all probability, she knew I would be opposed to plastic surgery in her case. And after such a long absence from therapy, she wasn't really my patient any more, so she didn't need my permission. Yet, she had greeted me enthusiastically and seemed happy about coming in.

Two days later, Julia arrived at my office, dressed in skin-tight, Lycra leggings that emphasized her protruding kneecaps and emaciated thighs. She tossed her long, black, curly hair, and the narrow streak of premature silver-gray that framed her left cheekbone glistened as she smiled broadly. "I was really looking forward to being here," were her opening words. Although she had made it clear that she was only coming for my "permission," inside I was humming. Individuals with anorexia are usually more attached to their disorders than they are to people. In order for them to give up that attachment, they need to replace it with another one. Julia's willingness to acknowledge that our relationship was important to her might be a sign that she was finally ready to break loose from the chains of her starvation.

It didn't take long for me to come back to reality: Being excruciatingly thin was still Julia's highest priority; it gave her life meaning. "I know it's stupid, but it's important to me," she said when I voiced my doubt that a flatter, ridgeless stomach would help her feel more comfortable with herself. Her only worry was how painful the surgery would be, not what wanting to have her stomach cut and sewn might say about her obsession with body image.

Nevertheless, as the session ended, Julia told me that she might, indeed, want to resume treatment at a later date. "My door is always open," I said, but as the words came out of my mouth, I knew that I might never see her again. Besieged by a stream of memories, I found myself reviewing our relationship.

"I'm petrified," she had said when she sat down in my office for the first time. "I have no control. My food is a mess. My mind is fuzzy and hazy."

Gaunt and listless as she was, Julia struck me as a bright, articulate 31-year-old who knew that she needed help. At 5'6", she weighed only 95 pounds. Although she claimed that her eating problem had started only six weeks earlier, I was skeptical. As it turned out, she had spent months secluded in her elegant, suburban ranch home, fasting, exercising, and struggling to cope with life. She was the mother of twin two-year-olds, a girl, Ashley, and a boy, Kyle—hard enough when you're properly nourished, but doubly daunting when you are lightheaded with hunger. In college, she said, she had weighed 125 pounds. Now, she couldn't imagine how she let herself weigh so much. Her goal was to reach 90 pounds. My heart dropped. Although she told me that she was scared by her perpetually tired and weak state, Julia was clearly more terrified of gaining weight. She restricted herself to a meager two bowls of cereal and a small salad a day, ran five miles every morning, and put herself through a strenuous two-hour aerobics workout five times per week. No wonder she wasn't feeling well! But when I explained to her that starvation has physiological consequences and can seriously affect the kidneys, brain, and heart, she tuned out. If getting better involved eating more, she wasn't interested. It was her twins that were tiring her out, not her skimpy diet, she insisted. So, as much as she said that she wanted help and had made her own decision to come to therapy, I wondered if Julia really did want to get better.

During that first session, I tried to gauge the severity of Julia's anorexia, but the picture that she gave me grew increasingly muddled. In answer to my questions about her running routine, she claimed that she didn't run if she was tired, but she hadn't missed a day of running in months. "Most people with 2-year-olds, much less twins, are tired a lot of the time," I commented, wanting to help her see how much she drove herself.

She smiled sweetly and acknowledged, "Yes, I guess you could say I exercise religiously."

In answer to my question about religion, I learned that Julia had grown up in a strict Catholic home. During the sessions that followed, I would notice how her language was imbued with concepts of guilt and pleasure, sin and suffering: "Eating gives me pleasure," she would say, "and that makes me feel guilty." At the time, I had no idea how complicated her relationship with her body really was.

"I get on and off the scale all day long," Julia told me. "All day" meant 10 or 15 times. When I asked her where she kept her scale, she lowered her eyes, smiled, and admitted that she had just moved it out of her bedroom. When I asked her why had she moved it, she replied, "Because I want to get it far from me." I was suspicious: Other patients move their scales from one room to another in order to weigh themselves in privacy, and often to hide their rituals from their husbands or family.

For some patients, these time-consuming rituals help to organize an inner chaos; others gain a sense of identity. In Julia's case, I suspected that both were true. New motherhood can feel overwhelming; it's hard to hold on to a sense of yourself, especially if you've given up your place in the work world in order to stay home with the kids. Julia had created her entire sense of self around thinness. And, I would quickly realize, her rituals distracted her from a pain far greater than hunger pangs.

"How does your husband feel about the weight you've lost?" I ventured.

"I don't think he realizes I have a problem," she said. Her husband, she added, was happy she was thin, because he had grown disgusted with his first wife when she gained weight after having kids. I was surprised at Julia's interpretation of her husband's failed marriage. 'Was there anything else going on with them?" I asked her. But Julia shook her head and stuck to her understanding.

Nevertheless, as we skimmed the surface of Julia's life during that first session, I felt reasonably optimistic. She was able to reflect on what we talked about and observe herself objectively. She told me that she was more obsessed with food since she'd been eating less, and I found her recognition of that fact encouraging. More encouraging still was her response to my question about why she might have become so obsessed with dieting. "Maybe staying home is part of it," she said.

But her answer to my next question, "What happened when you started staying home?" knocked the wind out of my sails. Suddenly, here was the Julia I had vaguely sensed: a woman filled to the depths with raw and agonizing feelings.

"I just slipped into a dark place," were her words. "I should be happy. I have two beautiful children who give me joy, I have a wonderful husband and a beautiful house. I should be happy, but I'm in a dark place, and that makes me feel guilty." I could have wept.

When Julia returned two days later, I learned more about her darkness. Because her weight was dangerously low, I had moved quickly to put together a treatment team consisting of a psychiatrist, a medical doctor, a nutritionist, and myself. Together, our job was to help keep her from sliding further downhill. But as the session progressed, my pessimism grew.

Once again, Julia began the session by telling me how hazy she felt, and how cold. I assured her that feeling cold was just another symptom of her anorexia. She was worried, too, about her children. She had left them with a babysitter, and was anxious that nobody but she could take proper care of them.

I was getting anxious, too, but for different reasons. She had all the characteristics of a hard-core anorexic, including the obsessiveness and the perfectionism. For the past few days, she had been a nervous wreck because her in-laws were coming to stay for the weekend. "Having overnight guests can be nerve-wracking, especially when you've got young children," I commented, wanting her to feel okay about the way she felt. But she bristled at my suggestion that she might feel anything but welcoming. That wasn't it.

"I'm terrified about eating in front of them," she told me. "I have the whole weekend planned—what I'll buy, make, bake. But I know I won't be able to eat."

'What is it that comes up for you when you think about eating?"

"A black wall."

"Can you see it?"

She could. In her mind's eye, she was sitting at the table. Everybody was eating, but she had to fake it. "I can't eat. The black thing blocks me off."

"Feel it blocking you," I prompted. "What does it feel like?"

"Hard. Cold. I feel it all though my body. I'm paralyzed. It's there when I open up the cabinets. It blocks me from eating anything except my comfortable bowl of cereal or salad . . . it's a very big block. It's thick. Very strong."

"How thick?" I asked her.

"One foot thick."

"Tell me more about it."

"It shields me from other people. It makes me uncomfortable."

"How long have you known your black wall?"

"Six weeks."

It had first appeared when a neighbor mentioned to Julia that she looked as if she was gaining weight. She remembered every detail of that day. She was home with the kids when the neighbor rang her doorbell and asked if she could pop in with her 4-year-old. Julia didn't want to say no. The children started running around, the house started to get into a state of disarray, and then the neighbor said it.

"My body froze," Julia recalled. "I felt nauseated, sick. Couldn't breathe. Didn't breathe…"

"And then?"

"Ever since that day—the wall."

Although Julia claimed that her black wall had appeared only recently, it didn't take long before we realized that she had been flirting with anorexia since her senior year of high school, when her boyfriend had dumped her for another girl. Once I understood that her problem was not only six weeks old, but was, in fact, chronic, the picture started to look gloomier.

Even as a child, Julia had rejected food as a way of expressing her anger when she felt neglected by her parents—a harsh, judgmental father and a cool, non-confrontational mother who would not stand in the way of Dad's tough parenting decisions. Instead of eating at the table with the family, Julia would lock herself in her room and go hungry. So, although the severity of her eating disorder was new, she had learned isolation and self-denial very early on. These lessons are fertile soil for anorexia.

Of course, not every child who locks herself in her room and refuses dinner develops an eating problem. Every parent knows that food is the number-one object in children's power struggles; many kids find that rejecting it is one of the few ways that, in the face of their powerlessness, they can claim some control over their lives. But as children grow up, parents typically loosen the reigns, letting them make mistakes, define their parameters, and learn their own lessons. Julia's parents, I would learn, had not.

I've always believed that telling the stories of our traumas is a pathway to healing. As we further explored Julia's childhood, one story in particular came up that seemed to have special significance for her because it represented all the times that her father had been harsh, cruel, and humiliating. One steamy June evening near the end of eighth grade, when she was hanging out on a corner with her friends, Julia had just lit up a cigarette, when a car approached them. It slowed down, and as it passed, she saw her father glaring at her through the open window. The veins on his head were standing out. He had caught her smoking and she knew she would pay.

When Julia got home just before her 11:00 curfew, both parents were waiting. Her father dragged her by the arm up the long, oak staircase to his bedroom, her mother close behind. Julia still remembered the click, click sound of their shoes as they climbed the wooden steps. When they got upstairs, her father locked the door. "If he had hit me with a belt it couldn't have been worse," Julia said, her eyes tearing. For two hours he lectured her about what a bad person she was. How could she disgrace herself? Where were her morals? Her Christian values? And the whole time that he was shouting his pronouncements, her mother stood by silently, neither participating, nor coming to her defense.

After that, Julia was grounded for weeks. She was not permitted to talk on the phone and was scarcely allowed to leave her room. Her parents spoke to her only when necessary, and her sister was not allowed to have anything to do with her. Julia felt as if she were in quarantine, as if she might contaminate anyone with whom she came into contact. She responded by refusing to eat. I wondered if this was where Julia's belief, "I must suffer," was born.

"It sounds as if your father used a sledgehammer to kill an ant," I said, "and after his tirade, there was little comfort from your mother."

"I was a wild child—a sinner," she replied. Clearly, Julia had taken her father's harsh judgment of her and made it her own. She was familiar with cruelty, pain, and starvation.

Another story stood out in one of our early sessions. We were exploring Julia's shame about her body, when I asked about her early sexual experiences. She told me, almost apologetically, that she'd first had sex when she was 14. She and her boyfriend were both drunk, and he forced her into it; she called the incident a "date-rape," as if the fact that it happened on a date made it both more tolerable and excusable. Afterwards, she went home and pretended that nothing had happened.

She continued to see her boyfriend, Jake, until he left her a few weeks later. They briefly got back together again in college—until he found Nicole, who was now his wife. I could only guess how guilty Julia must have felt about being drunk as a 14-year-old; how she'd blamed herself for what had happened.

"I would call that rape," I said. Although she had trivialized it by calling it a "date rape," I wanted her to consider that first sexual encounter for what it was—a damaging, traumatic experience that had left her vulnerable to an eating disorder. A large percentage of eating disorders are precipitated by cumulative trauma and body hatred that results from sexual abuse, but Julia seemed unable to feel for herself. "How would you feel if one of *your* daughters was date-raped?" I asked her. She couldn't respond. Even after we had returned to this incident many times, Julia only seemed to feel guilt and remorse for having been such a "bad" girl.

"By the time I was 14, I had no respect for my body. I deserved whatever happened to me. I deserved to have my body destroyed."

Like her father, she had learned to see punishment as the road to salvation; and, like her Pollyannaish mother, she couldn't stand up for herself. Better to pretend that everything was just fine.

Julia continued to tell many stories during our time together. A few months after beginning treatment, she joined an eating disorders therapy group that I led. Listening to the other women tell their tales helped her tell her own, and talking about her past did lead her to insights and even a temporary catharsis. But none of this seemed to do much to relieve her relentless commitment to losing weight, and she continued to be depressed.

I was concerned about this depression and consulted with Julia's psychiatrist, who re-evaluated the situation and prescribed a different antidepressant, as well as an anti-anxiety medication. Although at present there is no medication for anorexia nervosa, drugs can help a depressed or anxious patient to deal with moods.

Indeed, things soon seemed to take a turn for the better. Julia started to form a close bond with her nutritionist and was connecting to the other women in her eating disorders group. She found that she could learn a great deal from people with similar problems. When one member announced that she had managed to break off her relationship with her abusive boyfriend by "putting the group in my pocket when I went to meet him," Julia responded by saying, "I put the group in my pocket yesterday when I put sugar in my ice tea."

Our sessions, too, became more emotionally alive. Julia spoke less about food and weight and more about life at home with the twins. She complained about feeling trapped and stultified, and realized that for a long time she had felt suffocated by her husband and dutifully worked to keep his spirits up. Instead, he dragged hers down. I helped her work on feeling less responsible for him. Meanwhile, she looked into the idea of hiring a nanny and finding some type of work outside of the house. Given Julia's anxiety over leaving her children in a stranger's care, this was not an easy step for her to take, but she managed to take a part-time volunteer position in the pediatric unit of a local hospital.

Julia's first breakthrough came in February, when she took a trip to Florida. Taking the kids to visit her brother had been a big deal in itself, since she had never before left her husband at home and taken off on her own. Julia was exhilarated about exploring this new territory, rather than repeating the life of her mother, who had often complained about feeling "trapped" and had never gone anywhere alone. "A whole week by myself!" Julia exclaimed before she left.

The trip was better than either of us could have imagined. The next time I saw her, Julia told me that during the visit, she'd started writing in a journal, and in doing so had gained some insight into her eating problem. She had a shameful secret to tell me: She'd gotten herpes in college and had never told a soul. Throughout the last trimester of her pregnancy, she'd been terrified of having another outbreak. Even now, she was paying—her cesarean was necessitated more by the herpes than by the complications of a twin birth. "The scar of my twins is the scar of my mistake in getting herpes, but I didn't realize any of this was connected until I started writing. Now I realize that when I was pregnant, all of the guilt and shame I had hidden began to bother me. I just couldn't face any of it, so I decided that losing weight would help me feel better. Does that make sense?"

I assured her that it did. Often we distract ourselves from feeling badly any way we can. "You have a long history of feeling strong and powerful by refusing food," I reminded her. She agreed and added, "Dieting did more than help me feel strong. It was a way of dealing with the shame of getting a sexually-transmitted disease. I stopped eating in order to suffer."

"A lot of people have herpes," I told Julia in a matter-of-fact way, and encouraged her to share her secret in the group. She did, and was amazed to learn that another member had the same problem, and that another had had an abortion. "I guess nobody's perfect," she said.

When Julia and I talked about perfectionism, she realized that her parents had always demanded that she scored a hundred in everything she did. "Most of life is getting a B-plus," I told her. "Never letting yourself make a mistake can make you nuts."

She agreed. "Striving for perfection has been hard. When my neighbor said I was getting fatter, it was as if she was saying, 'You've made a big mistake.'"

A new page seemed to have turned in Julia's treatment. With all of the insights that she was developing and the way she "ate up" everything that went on in my office, I felt sure that the black wall that blocked her from eating would start to come down. She had even gained a little weight, when for no apparent reason, her wall suddenly reappeared.

One day, she came in and said, "I know I should feel happy, but I want to keep suffering. When I eat, a little voice tells me, 'You shouldn't have pleasure, you should have guilt.'" And she reiterated that she wanted to reach her goal of 90 pounds.

Looking back, I see clearly that I couldn't hear Julia when she insisted that she needed to keep losing weight. Was I suffering from a rescue fantasy? Did I think I could save her, even though she was telling me that she was not willing to get better?

Early in my training, one guideline that I had learned was to ask new patients if they were willing to gain five pounds to get better; those unwilling to even consider this small change had a guarded prognosis. Perhaps Julia's emotional growth sidetracked me from recognizing how stuck she was. In so many ways, she seemed to be finding her voice and living her life more fully. An actress in high school, she had even started taking private coaching sessions again and was about to try out for the local repertory company. Maybe I was seduced by her enthusiasm for all of the work we were doing in my office and in the group; she understood the dynamics that had shaped her and her eating problem. And just as we had developed a true fondness for each other, her relationships with friends, neighbors, and family seemed to expand, too.

Although on the one hand Julia's world was expanding, when it came to her eating, she seemed stuck—in fact, she was getting worse. After a six-week summer break, she showed up for our group therapy session shivering, and quickly wrapped herself in one of my hand-woven shawls. She had a foreboding piece of medical equipment attached to her chest. "It's a heart monitor," she said, the way one might speak about a new bathrobe. The other group members eyed the black band protruding from beneath her blouse. Were they feeling pity, I wondered? Fear? Both?

She had been away in the country, where, according to her, everything was "just fine" until the previous weekend, when she began to experience dizziness and a pressure in her chest. Her periods had recently stopped, and for a couple of weeks, she had been bursting into tears. "Medications don't work for me," she said. I knew that antidepressants sometimes help for a while and then lose their effectiveness. In retrospect, I wondered if Julia was sabotaging her progress by changing the dosages of her medication.

Hospitalization now loomed and I was in a deluge of calls with the other members of the treatment team. I was frightened. Although Julia's condition had not reached the point where the hospital was a medical necessity, her weight was dropping; she was now a pound lighter than when she entered therapy. Equally important, she was in a psychic jail, and nobody seemed to be able to find the key. I suggested that some intensive work in an inpatient treatment center might help extricate her from her stuck place.

Julia's response to the idea of hospitalization surprised me. While she was concerned about leaving her children, she wasn't opposed. In fact, she began to think of it as a "vacation" from the struggle to make herself eat.

And so, one Monday night during our regular group session, she stared down at the floor, anxiously winding long strands of black hair around her finger, and announced, "I'd like to start. I have something to tell you." The other six women turned their eyes towards her and waited. Finally, Julia spoke. After a great deal of soul searching, she said, she had made a decision to be hospitalized. She would be leaving for Florida early the following week. At first the room was silent. I wondered how the other members were reacting: With fear that her defeat was contagious? With envy that she had taken charge of her life?

Slowly, the other women spoke up, expressing concern, support, and hope: "Who will take care of your children?" "How has your husband handled this decision?" "What did your parents say?" "How are you with this decision?"

Julia's animated look reminded me of how nourishing caring conversation can be. The women's words, I noticed, fed her. I was aware, too, that I was adrift in an ocean of tumultuous feelings. First, I experienced relief and hope. In deciding to hospitalize herself, Julia expressed a willingness to reach out to others, to ask for help and connection. This is a major accomplishment for a person who has taken great pride in not needing anyone or anything, not even food, to stay alive. My heart was touched by the way Julia bravely announced this difficult decision and by the group members' responses. But behind my sense of relief lurked feelings of self-doubt and defeat. Neither my own efforts nor those of our team had helped her to crawl out of her agonizing abyss. What had gone wrong? What had she been too terrified to know?

"I have everything to live for," said Julia, "but..." Her voice trailed off. Silently I finished her sentence: a loving husband, two small children, a luxurious home, but in the midst of life's banquet, I am starving.

The day after Julia entered the hospital, I left on a trip to Costa Rica to visit my daughter, Rachel. I usually adore the solitude of a long plane ride, but this flight was different. I felt as though I was caught in an emotional no-man's land. On the one hand, I was filled with excitement about seeing Rachel, who had been backpacking around Latin America since her college graduation. And yet I found Julia's face haunting me. I felt that I had failed.

Of course, I should have known that feelings of depression and fatigue might set in. Hospitalizing a patient always wears me out, emotionally as well as physically. And I felt guilty. Julia was off "vacationing," as she called it, in the hospital, while I was off to sunny Costa Rica. Buckled in on the 727, my mind replayed our final goodbye— the hug as she left my office, the feeling of her fragile bones. She'd put her head on my shoulder, and the scent of her shampoo still lingered in my memory.

I found myself reviewing the team's decision: the calls back and forth in the late evening hours; the talks with the nutritionist and psychiatrist; the medical doctor's comment that hospitalization was not really a "medical necessity." And yet, Julia was not getting better. Perhaps the cloistered environment of an inpatient setting would offer her the safety she needed to dip deep into the place where it hurt, and would enable her to break the seal that kept her so isolated and untouched by us all. Maybe a new environment—something, someone, a whisper, a glance—would trigger something within her that would help her unlock the mystery of why she was firmly, relentlessly committed to weighing 90 pounds. As I sped toward Rachel, I worried and hoped for Julia.

Eighteen days in an inpatient program is not a long time. Before the days of managed care, most eating disorder patients were hospitalized for at least a month, and sometimes two. Nevertheless, her stay offered Julia an incredible amount of nourishment. She had entered weighing 94 pounds and came out at 102, looking renewed, more energetic, and healthier after eating 3500 calories a day. "I found a hole in that wall that allowed me to eat again!" she said proudly at our first session. She was committed to continuing her new eating plan, although she didn't yet know how difficult it would be without the "mealtime support." This cornerstone of the program had provided a staff member to sit with her during meals and help her to address the thoughts and feelings that blocked her from eating.

Just as important, I felt, was the fact that Julia had made some discoveries. Group sessions at the hospital encouraged her joyful self to emerge in a way that she could never have anticipated. She had also reached out to other patients in an effort to help them, and they had responded. She remembered that she used to have a lot of friends and realized that not only had anorexia become her best friend, it had completely taken over her life.

Going over the hospital report with Julia turned out to be a wonderful opportunity for collaboration. The staff had come to many of the same conclusions reached by our treatment team, which strengthened Julia's acceptance of what she had learned in my office. She was the child of rule-bound parents who didn't believe in showing their feelings, and her emotional development had been stunted; in order to recover, she needed to reclaim her feelings and voice. The report also confirmed Julia's sense that her inpatient experience had been a positive one. It gave a glowing summary of how much ground she had covered, how well she had related to both staff and patients alike, and how reflective she had been.

"Were you aware of all of this?" I asked.

In response, she revealed that she had stood up for herself a couple of times at the hospital. "I wasn't satisfied with the individual therapist they assigned me," she said. "At first, I just put up with her, but then I realized, I can do something about this, and I complained. Sure enough, they gave me someone new!" As I heard this, my heart leapt with optimism.

I should have known by now that for Julia, two steps forward might be followed by one step back. Within two weeks after returning home, she was having eating problems again. One of the hospital recommendations was that Julia join an intensive outpatient program, where she would have 10 hours a week of supervised meals and therapy. Julia went once and quit. Although she told me that the program wasn't right for her because the other women were all teenagers, I suspected that the idea of gaining yet more weight was simply too scary.

A line from Julia's discharge summary nagged at me: "She feared losing a sense of specialness that she associated with being thin." I tried to help her think about how else she could be special. "What does your husband think is special about you?" I asked her. "He thinks I'm a good mother and wife." When I asked her what that meant to her, she said, "I suppose, he means things like patient, caring, generous…" She had so many strong qualities, and yet she seemed only able to derive a sense of personal power or worth from thinness. It also remained her only measure of success.

Dark clouds were gathering, and the darkest arrived a couple of weeks later, when Julia came in and said, "I'm worried about Ashley. She's getting so flabby."

"Really?" I said, wondering how anyone could see a toddler as flabby, and alarmed by the fact that Julia was projecting her distorted sense of reality onto her daughter.

"She's a horrible eater. She loves sweets and potato chips. She hides candy upstairs in her room. I'm worried she'll get a round butt."

"And if she does?" I asked.

"Then the kids in school will tease her."

"Julia," I said, "I think children have far better things to think about than round butts." I wanted her to realize that the voice inside her head that told her she was fat had expanded its sphere and now was targeting her children as well. I warned her as gently as I could that parents pass on their anxieties about food and body image to their children. When we want our children to grow up feeling good about their bodies, we have to let them know in every way possible that what's inside of them matters most.

"You need to make it clear to your kids that people come in all shapes and sizes," I told her. "You are your children's most important teacher. They watch you eat and look at yourself in the mirror. They listen to what you say about your body and other people's bodies, as well." I described my experience with my children and how they were influenced by what I did: "When I smoked, no matter what I said about smoking, they learned that smoking was okay." She was surprised to learn that as a young mother, I felt a lot of shame about smoking in front of my children. "It's not what we say, it's what we do," I reminded her.

Among Julia's discharge recommendations were regular couples and family therapy, as well as continued individual and group sessions. Couples sessions were hardly more successful than the intensive outpatient therapy. Julia's husband, Nathan, came to the first session with an agenda: How could he help his wife eat? Julia had an agenda of her own. She wanted to take charge of her life and her eating. I tried to help Nathan accept that Julia was an autonomous being—that you can't control another person. He was frustrated. He wanted to help. "I'm great at problem solving, I'm not great at feelings," he said.

"It's great that you bring up these two issues," I told him, "because they're connected. Your wife isn't good at dealing with feelings, either, but she needs your support. She doesn't need you to solve her problem. Only she can determine her fate." Julia and Nathan canceled their second appointment. He didn't want to come back, and she didn't want to push him.

I had an opportunity to meet Julia's parents in a family session when they were visiting for the twins' birthdays. Immediately, a gulf opened between them. Julia wanted her parents to understand the agony of her struggle; they wanted her to know that they loved her. "We just want you to be better," her mother kept saying. Her father said, "Just tell me what you need." I wanted Julia to speak up and tell them, but, as always it seemed, her parents could not talk or hear about "bad" things. They wondered why she was crying so much, but they didn't really want to know the answer. They just wanted her tears to stop.

"I thought they'd understand that my suffering is not about food, but they don't get it," Julia told me. "The person that's inside me—they don't see her. When I'm with them, I'm invisible. It's unbearable."

I felt for her. "People think they can help by trying to change you," I explained. "Sometimes the most important change is that you understand each other. Regardless of whether or not your parents understand or support you, though, you can still be you."

I ask myself, now, whether I should have pushed harder for more couples and family therapy. Julia wanted the people closest to her to know and accept the whole of her—her pain, her conflicts, her needs. Only then could she truly be the person that she was discovering in my office. "I speak my true self here, but I'm not true to myself outside of here," Julia once told the other women in the group. Once again, she felt she was up against a wall—her parents and her husband wanted to save her; they didn't want to know her pain. I was up against a wall, too. You can't make an adult patient, or her family, do what they don't want to do.

As the months rolled on, every time I thought about the enigma of Julia, I came back to her rape. Yet, no matter how often I brought it up, she minimized its importance. Then, one evening near the end of her second year of treatment, she surprised me by bringing a dream into our group session that clearly linked that event and her eating disorder.

"It's a very weird dream," she began. "I'm in a room with Jake." Julia turned to Tami, the newest member of the group. "He's the guy that raped me." Then she continued in the same matter-of-fact tone. "It's a very short dream. I'm in his apartment and we just got off the bed, and who's there but Nicole, the girl he dumped me for and ended up marrying. She is so fat . . . and I am so thin. And I'm smiling and gloating, thinking how jealous she is of me."

I was shuddering when Julia finished. Here she was, talking about a rape and a rejection that still haunted her after more than two decades, and yet, from the flat way she spoke, you would have thought that nothing bad had happened. I flashed back to her mother sitting in my office, glossing over Julia's pain with the words, "We just want you to know that we love you, dear," and Julia's comment: "My mother is happy as long as we stay with the facts." I shuddered again. I was feeling what Julia, who had deadened herself to a range of intolerable emotions, could not feel.

Although Julia and I had been over her rape dozens of times, I saw a new chance for healing here in the group. Perhaps she would benefit from hearing the reactions of the other women. "Tami, you look a bit off," I said. "What's happening inside you?"

Tami turned to Julia. "You were raped?" she asked, wide-eyed. Julia nodded. "Oh my God," Tami said. "I had no idea."

"What are you feeling about this? What does your 'oh my God' mean?" I asked Tami.

"I don't know," she replied. "I was never raped. But Julia, you're talking about it in such a nonchalant way!" I was overjoyed. Tami had pinpointed Julia's problem and given it a new name. Maybe now, Julia could acknowledge that she was dissociated from her pain, and that her inner life was damaged by a darkness she had not wanted to illuminate.

"Well," said Julia, "it was more than 20 years ago."

"Twenty years ago!" exclaimed Tami. "How old were you?" When Julia told her 14, I noticed tears in Tami's eyes.

Other women in the group had questions, too. Meagan wanted to know if Julia had confided in anyone at that time because she knew that silence would mean a double trauma. Being raped was the first, not being comforted was the second. Meagan understood only too well. She had been mugged at knifepoint as a teen and had suffered the humiliation of having her experience erased with the words, "What's the big deal?" and "You'll get over it."

I could feel a sense of horror growing in the room. "Fourteen," I said slowly, addressing myself to all of the women. "See yourselves at 14." Looking around me at the women, each lost in her personal recollections, I had my own fleeting memory of being at a drive-in movie with a boy who had groping hands. I remembered what it was like to fend off sexual advances at that age, and the awkwardness of my adolescence flooded me.

I looked at Julia, who, it turned out, was still immersed in her dream. She broke the silence with, "In my dream, Nicole is just standing there, glaring at me. She glares, and I feel triumphant. She is so damn envious of me. Look at me, how thin I am!"

"I brought in a poem that reminded me of you," I told Julia at the beginning of her next session, and handed her a copy of "Slipping Through the Cracks," by Leslea Newman. The poem expresses the self-blame, shame, and erosion of self-worth that many adolescent girls experience when they realize that their blossoming bodies render them powerless prey. Then, instead of celebrating, girls swallow their pride, silence their once-strong voices, and try to disappear.

I suggested that Julia read the poem aloud, hoping that she would identify with the theme and feel compassion for herself. She began in her soft, Southern drawl:

The air was thick with the promise

of lilacs that evening
and the clouds hovered around my shoulders
like the mink stole in my mother's closet
I tried on from time to time.
I was sixteen and I knew it.
I tossed my head like a proud pony
my hair rippling down my back in one black wave
as I walked down the sultry street
my bare feet barely touching the ground
past the sounds of television,
a dog barking,
a mother calling to her child,
my body slicing through the heavy air
like a sailboat gliding on lazy waters.

When the blue car slowed alongside me
I took no notice
until two faces leaned out the open window
"Nice tits you got there, Honey."
"Hey, Sweetheart, shine those headlights over here."
"Want to go for a ride?"
I stopped,
dazed as a fish thrust out of water
into sunlight so bright it burns my eyes,
I turn and walk away fast,
head down, arms folded,
feet slapping the ground,
"Nice ass, too," they call
and then I hear laughter
the screech of tires
silence…

All at once I feel ashamed of my new breasts
round as May apples,

I want to slice them off with a blade
sharp as a guillotine.
All at once I am ashamed of my widening hips
I want to pare them down with a vegetable peeler
until they are slim and boyish.
All at once I want to yank out my hair by the roots
like persistent weeds that must not grow wild.
But I am a sensible girl.
I do none of these things.

Instead I go home, watch TV with my parents
brush my teeth and braid my hair for the night.
And the next day I skip breakfast
eat an apple for lunch
and buy a calorie counter,
vowing to get thinner and thinner
until I am so thin I can slip
through the cracks in the sidewalk
and disappear. And I do.

"I really feel sad for that girl," Julia said as she finished reading the poem. "She was filled with self-hate."

"And you? How do you feel for yourself?" I asked. I wasn't surprised to hear her answer: "What about me?" I was filled with gloom. Julia was committed to deadness, and she had almost deadened me.

During the following weeks, Julia fired one after another member of her treatment team: first the psychiatrist, then the medical doctor, and finally the nutritionist. I was surprised, for in her own way, Julia had developed a close relationship with each of them. She disagreed when I commented on this. She said that she was disappointed and that taking charge of her life was "long overdue." Although she insisted that she would remain in therapy with me, I was waiting for my walking papers. When she told me that she and her husband would be spending the summer months in the mountains and we would have to continue her individual therapy by phone, I was surer than ever that I would be the next to go. So, when she returned in September and called to tell me that she had decided to take a break, I was not really surprised. It took my best efforts to convince her to come in one more time, just to say goodbye.

Julia walked in with a big smile. "You'll be pleased for me, I hope," she said, and started cataloguing how well her life was going. She was still doing volunteer work, but had also decided to begin a graduate program in early education, starting course work in a few weeks. The contractor she had hired to build a new wing on her house had quit, but, "I know there are others." I was pleased to hear her sound so relaxed about a situation that, at another time, might have panicked her. She'd spent the summer growing closer to her parents, who visited for a month. "They have their limitations, but they do love me, and I realize that I have to accept them for who they are," Julia said. She had also made friends with other women in her community and, in their company, had enjoyed simply being herself. "I wasn't a patient to my new friends," she told me. She was sick of the old, "Hi everyone, I'm Julia, I'm an anorexic," and claimed that, "If you don't identify yourself as an anorexic, you're just a person."

She sounded fed up with therapy and doctors, and I could understand why. For two years, her life had been consumed with office visits, but she was still terrified to eat. Of course she was discouraged. Although I didn't agree, she kept insisting that perhaps she just needed a break, but when our session was coming to a close, she told me, "My husband thought you would try to talk me into staying." I didn't know if she was relieved or disappointed that I hadn't.

She was already on her way out of my office when she turned to me and said, "I know I still have issues." I waited, sensing that she had more to say, and hoping that maybe, in these last moments, she might finally be ready to reconsider her decision to leave. Looking at her standing with her hand on the door handle, her body impossibly frail under her jogging suit, I realized how deeply I had come to care for her and how much I wanted her to be whole and healthy.

Then she dropped the bomb. The previous week, she said, she had gone swimming in the ocean near her home, even though the red flags were signaling a hurricane warning. She almost drowned. The life-guards had to pull her out of the water and give her mouth-to-mouth resuscitation, while her family looked on from the huge crowd that had gathered.

With a lump in my throat, I asked her, "What is the message you gave your husband and children and are now giving me?" She shrugged, looked into my eyes, and said, "For a moment, I wished I could have been swept into the sea and it would be all over."

We stood in silence for what seemed like a long time before I reached out and touched her hand. "I'm sure you'll come back when you are ready."

I believed what I was telling her—that one day, she would be ready and she would call. Never in my wildest dreams did I imagine that the next time I heard from her, she would be planning to have plastic surgery to remove the scar from the birth of her twins, which for her represented guilt, shame, and self-hatred.

Ever since Julia left my office to have her "ridge" removed, I've asked myself, *What went wrong? What did I miss? Would another therapist have done a better job?* It's still a mystery to me. I always believed that emotional suffering arises from profound disconnection from oneself, others, and the universe. The goal of therapy is to repair these broken bonds by helping patients develop their capacity to love and experience joy. Ironically, this means helping them dip into their unmet hungers—their pain.

What puzzled me was that Julia remained stuck despite the fact that so much of the necessary repair work that should have occurred in her treatment did. I had reached out to her with all that I felt, and she seemed to respond by opening her heart to me. She learned to feel for and connect with others in her life. She even allowed herself to take the difficult step of accepting that her parents had not been there for her in all the ways she needed. Although she had made so many gains, she left therapy as obsessed with being thin as when she entered. Her attachment to her eating disorder remained greater than her attachment to me. "It's part of my life and it probably always will be," she told me in our last session.

Then, a short time after Julia left my care, something happened in the therapy group that made me think of her again. Diana had arrived with a poem. "I'd like to start," she said as she passed out copies of a typed page. "Someone gave me this poem at an Overeaters Anonymous meeting. It's called, 'Don't Change.'" All eyes were on her as she read:

I was a neurotic for years.
I was anxious and depressed and selfish.
Everyone kept telling me to change.

I resented them and I agreed with them,
And I wanted to change, but simply couldn't,
No matter how hard I tried.

What hurt the most was, that like the others,
My best friend kept insisting
That I change.
So I felt powerless and trapped.

Then one day, he said to me:
"Don't change . . .
I love you exactly as you are."

Those words were music to my ears:
"Don't change . . . don't change . . . don't change.
I love you as you are."

I relaxed. I came alive. And suddenly, I changed!

Now I knew that I couldn't really change until I found
someone who would love me whether I changed or not.

My heart skipped a beat as Diana read and Julia's voice reverberated within me. Had I tried too hard to change her? Had I grown too attached to the idea of healing her?

Ever since Diana read that poem, I've kept a copy of it in the back of my appointment book. It reminds me that sometimes I should give up the struggle and let a patient cling to her eating disorder, accepting her for who she is even while I hope that someday she can be more. I must sit tight and wait, and resign myself to the fact that while anorexia or bulimia limit a person, they also help her to deal with and survive her life. In the end, I must accept the fact that many people with eating disorders continue to lead quite functional lives despite their ongoing struggles.

At times, even after 20 years of being a therapist, I'm still bewildered. When a patient doesn't recover, I'm left with feelings of wonder, as well as regret. I try not to blame myself or my patients and accept that some people are able to relinquish their attachment while others cannot. I'm still looking for answers: heredity, biochemistry, genetic predisposition. Recently, I've been looking at research suggesting that early maltreatment, whether it is physical, sexual, or emotional, has enduring negative effects on brain development. Perhaps one day we'll better understand why therapy proves ineffective for some people. Or is my search for answers just another way of not facing the fact that eating disorders, like any other psychological problem, exist in a continuum; some are more severe than others, and some people are more resistant to change?

It's hard to face the reality that I didn't make a difference—or, at least, not the one that I wanted. Maybe our relationship did matter more than I will ever know—perhaps it helped her survive. Sometimes, as I sit in my office and go over these questions in my mind, my eyes land on the knitted shawl that I keep draped over the chair, and I remember Julia sitting there, shivering, wrapped in its warmth.

7

The Frozen Sea Within

Writing is an axe to break the frozen sea within.
—Franz Kafka

When I was 12, my grandmother took me to see the Broadway production of *The Diary of Anne Frank*. Sitting in the dark, I was mesmerized by the earnest, scared girl, hiding from the Nazis, whose body was trapped in a teeny space. By the time the knock came on the annex door and the curtain fell, I was overcome with grief. The next day I began my first journal.

As I grew up, writing was one way I had of caring for myself, of feeling safe when I was lonely or scared. Diaries, then spiral notebooks, and eventually more elegant, cloth-covered books gave voice to inner musings, psychic struggles, joy, and suffering.

In Freshman English 101, Professor O'Hara, a tall, imposing man with a woolly beard, opened our first class with, "We read to know we are not alone, we write to find ourselves." His words made a powerful impression on my young mind and inspired me to begin a quote journal in which I recorded and mulled over what I felt were words of inspiration from great thinkers, poets, or Professor O'Hara. I later became an English teacher, and sharing my passion for reading and writing became my mission—no easy task, considering that my students were poor readers and hated writing.

"Why do we have to write?" they would ask. There is something about writing it down that is different than talking it out. Writing helps you build trust in your ideas and beliefs. It makes you dig deep inside yourself and connects you to your internal life.

Because writing has enabled me to know myself in a unique way, it's no wonder that when I became a psychologist, I wove it into my work with patients, especially with eating disordered teenagers. Anyone who has tried to reach the inner world of a young anorexic or bulimic by talking knows how frustrating it can be. Journal writing provides another way of opening the door and looking inside.

Such was the case with Becky Andover, who first came to see me at age 15, locked in what seemed to be an impenetrable world of carefully measured calories. She was referred to me by her school psychologist, Dr. Elyssa Barnett. "She can *really* use your help," Dr. Barnett told me over the phone. Her emphasis on the word "really" left me with an uncomfortable feeling.

Apparently, three of Becky's friends had approached Dr. Barnett because they were alarmed by the fact that she looked so thin yet spoke of herself as fat, never ate with them in the cafeteria, and claimed to be too busy studying to return their phone calls or hang out after school. Listening to Dr. Barnett's account, I was struck by how odd this situation was; usually a teenager's parents, not her friends, are the worried ones.

When I received Dr. Barnett's call in September, Becky, at 5'5", weighed 98 pounds; she had lost 16 pounds during the summer. By the time she came to see me in October, she was a frail-looking 96 pounds— a half-child, half-wizened woman, who sat in my office tapping her foot incessantly. Her shoulders were stooped, her chest sunken, her hair thin and unkempt. It had taken her a whole month to get into my office because her mother had canceled two previous appointments, the first because Becky had to go to a gymnastics meet, and the second because her mother had an unexpected out-of-town business meeting. Both times, the unspoken message was clear: Therapy can wait. Dr. Barnett had warned me about that, too. "Getting her into your office may be difficult," she'd told me. "Her mother's just getting back on her feet after a nasty divorce. Her father remarried recently, and goes away on business a lot. Neither parent is easy to reach."

I glanced at Becky sitting upright in her chair, looking like a forlorn child awaiting punishment. "I'm very, very sorry, but my mother's train was late and then there was a lot of traffic," she began. *Why apologize when the delay wasn't her fault?* I wondered. Was she always so anxious to smooth things over?

"I'm glad we are finally able to meet," I replied. She responded with a smile, a tap, and a shrug, tossing the ball back in my court. I tried again. "I wonder how you feel about being here?"

Another shrug. "Just fine."

"Your friends have been worried about you."

"That's silly." Tap, tap. I would soon observe that this girl's body was in constant motion. Was she afraid that upsetting thoughts or feelings would erupt if she sat still?

"Do you know why they're worried?" She shook her head. While I am skilled at going slowly and establishing trust with a new patient, Becky's fragile appearance reminded me that there was no time to waste. I took the plunge. "Your friends are worried that you are anorexic." No response, except for the tapping foot. Had I made a mistake in bringing up the anorexia so soon? "What do you think of your friends' concern?"

"Anorexics are thin, and I'm anything but thin," she said. "It doesn't matter how little I eat, I can't lose enough weight."

"Enough weight?"

"I want to lose enough to stop thinking about losing any more."

"And how much weight is that?"

Becky shrugged, tapped, and said sweetly, "I don't know."

"When did you become so concerned with your weight?"

Becky sat up, stopped tapping, and began to talk in a more animated way. Her story was all too familiar. "I've always had a big butt," she said, "and last spring I decided to do something about it." She went on a diet and joined the track team. After track she would exercise for another hour. "Now I exercise after I eat anything."

"What's anything?"

"Even if I eat a few carrots or an apple, I have to do sit-ups."

"How many?" I asked. Becky did sets of 100. "What happens if the phone rings or you lose count?" I anticipated her answer. If her routine was interrupted, she would have to start over. She wasn't sure why, but no less than exactly 100 at a time would do.

Sit-ups were only one of many rituals controlling her life. She ate breakfast by 7 A.M. and dinner by 7 P.M. and consumed no more than 300 calories at any meal. She allowed herself three daily snacks, but only fifty calories per snack. Often I have heard from patients about specific numbers having magical properties. How easy it is to rely on a number when your life turns upside down, as I assumed was the case with Becky.

"Tell me about the snacks. Do you have them at set times? Or can you have them whenever you choose?"

"Set times. A quarter after the hour and only odd hours: eleven, one, and three o'clock."

And so it went. At an age where most girls are preoccupied with friendships, cliques, and boys, Becky's waking hours were devoted to thinking about what she would, should, and could eat, how many calories she consumed, and how much she would have to exercise to avoid gaining an ounce.

Even before I met Becky, Dr. Barnett's brief description suggested to me that this girl was anorexic. The restricted eating and weight loss, intense fear of becoming fat, and social isolation and withdrawal all pointed to it. Now, as I listened to Becky describe her rituals around eating and exercise, I also began to suspect an obsessive-compulsive component.

People who suffer from Obsessive-Compulsive Disorder, or OCD, are plagued by obsessive, worrisome thoughts, and in fact, anorexia and OCD frequently occur together. While all of us worry, people with OCD can't turn their worries off except by focusing on another thought, like their weight, or by engaging in some type of compulsive behavior, like dieting. Becky counted calories and sit-ups the way, I would later learn, she had stacked and counted her pennies when she was little. As she sat in my office, tapping her foot and breezily detailing her dieting regime, I wondered what agonizing thoughts she might be trying to banish.

"It wasn't always like this," Becky answered in response to my question about how long she had been such a strict dieter. "I can still remember that 'other' me." A touch of sadness hung in the room as she told me about her life only a year earlier, when she looked forward to eating pizza and cake at her best friend's birthday party.

"What happened to that 'other' you? Where did she go?" Again Becky shrugged and tapped. She had no idea how or why her former self had disappeared. "Anything unusual happen last year when you started that diet?" Nothing she could think of. Tap, tap. "Wasn't that when your father remarried?" I asked, recalling my conversation with Dr. Barnett. Becky nodded. "How was that for you?" I asked.

Without skipping a beat, she replied, "I'm happy for my Dad! And I just love his new wife."

"How nice," I said to her. *Ouch!* I said to myself.

Our session was coming to a close. "I'll tell you what I'm thinking," I said. "It sounds like you've lost part of who you are." She nodded. "Whenever we lose parts of ourselves, there's a reason. But that 'other' you *is* still inside. If you're interested, we can try to find her."

A smile spread across Becky's face. "Okay," she said.

After she left, I took stock of the situation. Becky certainly appeared to be at risk. Her weight was dropping and her medical profile was precarious, yet I felt hopeful. The very fact that she could recall a symptom-free existence was a positive sign. Many of my patients can't remember life before their symptoms, but Becky was in touch with that "other" person. I hoped I might help her reclaim her capacity to live in a more nourishing way, and free herself from the crippling obsessive thoughts, feelings, and rituals that accompany anorexia.

First, I needed to create a treatment team, and the best teams always include parents. I called both Becky's mother and father and left messages on their answering machines that were clear and to the point: "I need your help." For the first session, we would all meet together. Joint sessions tend to expose family issues and point out the problems that lurk beneath an eating disorder. However, too much conflict might get in the way of creating a safe climate where feelings could be freely aired and relationships healed. If the atmosphere was too emotionally charged—typical in cases of divorce—I would design another format.

Since professional collaboration not only heals patients, but supports therapists as well, my next calls were to a physician and a nutritionist with whom I had worked successfully in the past. Even though it was too early to know if I needed to include a psychiatrist on the team, I mentally flipped through my Rolodex in search of one I might consult in the future, should medication also seem appropriate. While anorexia is generally unresponsive to medication, the opposite is true of OCD.

Two days later, Becky returned. Our first session had focused mainly on her obsession with losing weight. I felt sure that if I gently probed, she would loosen up and reveal something of herself. Unfortunately, I was in for another reminder about how difficult she was to reach.

"What can you tell me about your mom?"

"She's the greatest!" Her foot started tapping.

"How do you two get along?"

"Really fine."

"What kinds of things do you two do together?"

"Oh, she doesn't have much time for me. Since the divorce, she works all the time. I feel really bad for her. She has to get up so early to commute into New York City, and she works so late that we don't really see much of each other at night." Tap, tap.

"What's it like, being alone so much?"

"I try to help her out with cleaning up and cooking. Last night I made a brisket." I noticed how Becky had avoided answering my question.

Since therapy is a process of learning to honor our hungers, and I hoped that eventually I could help Becky acknowledge her hunger for a caring relationship, I started by honoring her most basic hunger: for food.

"So, you made a nice dinner for your Mom. How considerate!" I said, thinking about how much Becky took care of and fed her mother while she starved herself. "What was dinner like?"

"Oh, we didn't have dinner together. She had to work late so she grabbed a bite with a friend and I ate by myself," she said, cheerily. Tap, tap. My heart sank.

"I see," I said, feeling sad at the thought of Becky sitting alone at the kitchen table, probably barely touching her food.

"What time is your mom coming home tonight?"

A shrug and a tap. "I never know. I just wait and see."

Regardless of how direct I was, Becky revealed nothing of her feelings. *Back off for now,* I reminded myself. When I inquired about her father, Becky gave a repeat performance. She told me that he was happily remarried and living an hour away in Connecticut. He, too, didn't have much time for her, but she understood how busy he was.

"Does he come out to Long Island to see you?" I asked.

"Oh no, I go to Connecticut to see him. The problem is, he just moved into a very small apartment—that's all he can afford. It's a one bedroom with a sleep couch in the living room, so there's not much room for me to stay over." Tap, tap.

I kept trying. "And his new wife, Evvie," I said. "Last time, you said how much you liked her. What about her do you especially like?"

Becky shrugged. "Everything," she said flatly.

By the third week, Becky was seeing the team physician and nutritionist regularly. Her physician told me that, even though she was following the meal plan she had worked out with her nutritionist, she was still losing weight and was at a critical point. However, since her heart rate, electrolytes, kidneys, and other internal organ functions were normal, her condition wasn't life-threatening; we agreed that at this point she didn't require hospitalization.

Nevertheless, I was worried. Although Becky was still functioning in her daily life—getting up in the morning, going to school, keeping up with her homework—I knew that we were in a race against time, one that I feared we might lose. Our conversations remained focused on her fears about eating and getting fat. Every session had the same motif: Everything is fine—mom, dad, even the divorce. No problems. How would I reach the frozen place inside Becky?

That night I had a dream. I was on a frozen pond I used to love as a child, skating around and around on what I knew was thin ice. The surface cracked and I started to fall into the freezing water. Terrified, I tried to grab something solid with my free hand and pull myself out, but the crack was getting bigger. Then I saw Becky, half-submerged. My other hand was locked in hers, trying to lift her, and I woke up with the realization that I was trying to stop myself from being pulled under as Becky's weight slipped.

While driving to a meeting early the next morning, I thought about the dream and felt a knot in my stomach. Becky *was* skating on thin ice, and so was I. I remembered how hard it had been for me, as a 15-year-old, to tell anyone about the things that bothered me. I couldn't reveal my scariest thoughts to my best friend, much less open up to a virtual stranger. But I had my journal into which I had poured all my innermost feelings.

I recalled Becky mentioning during one of our first sessions that she was a writer of sorts and enjoyed making lists in her diary—homework, money she owed and what was owed to her, and, of course, food and calories. Franz Kafka's words hummed in my ear: "Writing is an axe to break the frozen sea within." Becky couldn't talk to me about her feelings, but she might develop some connection to them if she started to write. By seeing her ideas on the printed page, she might be able to stand back and think about what she was doing. She might even develop an awareness of her deeper hungers. I also wondered if writing and sharing her words during our sessions might help Becky develop a connection to me as well as to herself.

I remember you like to write," I said to Becky at our next session. She beamed. I wasn't sure if it was because she loved writing or was simply pleased that I remembered this detail. I told her that I love to write, too; that writing is a way people get to know themselves better.

Because she had been following her nutritionist's instructions to keep track of what she ate, I said to her, "Let's go a step further. I have a hunch if you write down your thoughts and feelings, as well as your foods, we might get a better idea of what's going on and why you're not gaining weight." My casual instructions spawned a rash of questions about exactly what she was to write about.

"There's no right and wrong," I assured her, and opened my supply closet, took out a blank spiral notebook, and handed it to her. "You don't have to be perfect." I kept the guidelines vague on purpose. I wanted to challenge her rigid style of thinking and help build her confidence in herself and her intuition. It was my way of saying, *Take a chance. Your way is okay with me.* I wondered how she would take my suggestion. Would she feel helped and supported or controlled by me?

Becky arrived at her next session and asked enthusiastically, "Would you like to see my notebook?" I felt as if she was giving me a gift.

"Of course," I said. I leafed through the first few pages, noting the meticulous handwriting, and handed the notebook back to her. "It would be best if you read it aloud to me," I suggested, knowing that in reading her own words, she would achieve a greater level of self-awareness. Becky read:

> *Breakfast:*
> *Cup of black coffee.*
> *Bagel without dough with veggie cream cheese.*

Bowl of Fiber One with half a banana.
Will I gain weight from this? It hurts when I eat.

First, I praised her efforts: such a cooperative observer! *How perfect this task is for an obsessive, compliant person,* I thought. Next, using her journal, I tried to forge a deeper relationship with her.

"It hurts when you eat," I said, hoping to connect her to inner wounds that were both hidden and expressed by her disordered eating. Becky nodded. "Where?" She pointed to her stomach. I continued to ask questions about the nature of this discomfort, hoping to draw her attention to both her physical and psychic pain. "Does your hurt come and go or is it a constant?" "Is the pain sharp or dull and throbbing?" "Is it triggered by eating the bagel? The Fiber One? Or by drinking coffee?" I wanted to show her that in our relationship, her needs mattered and could be voiced; that what she thought, felt, and did touched me.

Becky shrugged. The pain was vague. She looked at the floor. I tried to stay attuned to her concerns, however, and she eventually rewarded me with details about the bagels she ate, the cream cheese that she craved, and how hard she had searched to find the "right" low-fat brand.

"*Craving* cream cheese," I said, emphasizing the word "craving," with the hope that Becky would take in the word's double meaning and see that other unarticulated longings and desires lay beneath the surface. "Craving anything else?" I asked, but she shrugged, tapped, and looked away.

I was fairly sure that Becky's anorexia and obsessive-compulsive behaviors had been triggered by her father's remarriage—the timing was too obvious to ignore. Like many children of divorce, she had probably struggled with all kinds of feelings when her parents separated: rejection, abandonment, and uncertainty about the future. While the chaos of divorce intensifies a child's wish for security and guidance, separating parents rarely provide those because they are in the process of discarding the routines and rituals that held together their marriage and family. They can get swept away by the thrill of liberation and are eager to explore their new independence. Becky may have secretly harbored the dream that her parents would reconcile and family life would go back to its old ways. Dreams can stave off anxiety; remarriage dashes them. Becky's obsessive worries about being fat could be one way to control her pain, anxiety, and anger.

"I've worked with tons of kids and heard lots of stories about divorce," I ventured. "From what I understand, the breakup of a family is never easy. What was your parents' divorce like for you?"

"I felt bad when Dad moved to Connecticut."

"It sounds like it was hard on you." Becky nodded.

"Did he know how you felt?"

"Of course! I told him I missed him, but he told me that I'd get over it. And you know what? He was right! I know that he loves me and I love him, and I really understand that he had to do what was best for him."

"How understanding you are," I said. *How much you need to protect yourself*, I thought. It was as if she were in a powerful hypnotic trance that decreed: You *must* keep all negativity out of your consciousness! One negative thought might lead to another, and another and another— and will take you right back to those unbearable feelings.

Becky's parents cancelled our first joint appointment. I understood that their schedules were crowded with professional and personal commitments, but in the series of phone messages that surrounded the rescheduling, I got a dose of what I imagined she suffered most of the time—feeling like an inconvenience and a burden.

When her parents finally did come in, our session painted a painful landscape of Becky's early life. Linda and Gregory were trim and meticulously-groomed people who still presented themselves as the enviable "perfect couple" they were when they first met in high school. After graduating college, Greg had joined his father's thriving lumber business and Linda, an elementary school teacher, had decorated their new home. They described their early years as "charmed."

The conception, pregnancy, birth, and infancy of their firstborn, Jared, followed effortlessly. But this perfect existence left them unprepared for what came next: two miscarriages and, when Jared was six, the death of their second child just five days after her birth. She was buried nameless. Her death plunged Linda into the depths of desolation.

Tragedy, says a Chinese proverb, brings us to a crossroads where the fork of danger meets the fork of opportunity. It compels some people to turn to friends for support and comfort, while others withdraw. I imagined that after the baby's death, neither Linda nor Greg could express their sorrow; instead, both became busier than ever. On a conscious level, neither wanted to burden the other. On a deeper level, neither could tolerate their feelings of loss. A state of emptiness ensued, enveloping each of them and their relationship. It was into this barren and devitalized world that Becky was born, two years after the death of the baby girl.

Becky was unplanned, and her birth premature. For months after the Cesarean, Linda remained bedridden and depressed while Becky was cared for by a succession of nannies who complained about the colicky baby who was difficult to feed and cried continuously.

Linda and Greg recounted the tragedies of their lives together, including the divorce, without a trace of sadness. They were strangers to their emotional lives. And while both expressed concern about Becky's weight loss, neither seemed struck by a sense of urgency or dismayed in the face of imminent hospitalization. They were as good at distancing themselves from their daughter's tragedy as they were from their own. Becky had learned well from them.

Wanting to involve them in Becky's care, I asked questions: What did they understand about her eating disorder? Had they spotted any warning signs or observed anything different about her? Similar to Becky's responses in our early sessions, neither parent had much to say, so I changed tactics and tried to educate them.

"Everyone who wants to be thin doesn't develop an eating disorder," I explained, adding that eating disorders are usually a way of coping with difficult emotional struggles. "Although you two are handling your divorce, it may be more disturbing to Becky than either she or you realize." From her father's response, I wasn't sure that he had heard my hint, which made me wonder whether he heard Becky.

"Even though she's seen you for a few weeks," he said, "she's still worried about her weight. It's silly, seeing how thin she is."

"Telling her that her worries are silly isn't going to help her feel close to or understood by you. It will just be frustrating," I said, "and it won't keep her from dieting. Or worrying." I told him that a serious eating disorder takes a long time to develop and a long time to heal, and in Becky's case, part of the healing process would involve shoring up her shaky sense of self.

"You can help by being a good listener and being patient, " I suggested. Linda and Greg were nodding in unison. I had expected questions; neither asked any, so I continued by explaining Becky's vicious cycle of obsessive thoughts and compulsive behaviors.

"Psychiatrists sometimes categorize patients with common OCD behaviors as 'counters,' 'cleaners,' 'checkers,' and 'hoarders,'" I said. "Do you remember Becky doing any of these things when she was little?" Linda told me about Becky's penny counting. "Is there a history of anything like this in either of your families?" They shook their heads.

"We can never be sure what has triggered her eating disorder," I told them, "but my guess is that she may have a vulnerability to OCD. Some people are born with a chemical imbalance, a predisposition for OCD. The obsessive thoughts are triggered when something stressful happens in life. A switch goes off in the brain. This switch can be tripped by something as incidental as a virus, by emotional stress, or by a traumatic event like your divorce. There's always a rush at OCD clinics after a serious earthquake." I explained that the two common treatments for OCD were psychotherapy and medication.

"In Becky's case," I told them, "I want to hold off on medication for now and see how we do with therapy." I didn't see the point of exposing a 15-year-old to the side-effects of medication unless it became absolutely necessary. "What will help your daughter most is your interest in her life. Spend time with her. Find things you enjoy doing together that don't have to do with food, exercise, or dieting.

When it comes to food, you would help her by offering to sit with her while she eats. Also, you can limit the number of choices at each meal so that you don't feed her tendency to fuss over what to eat."

As the weeks slipped by, Becky seemed comfortable recording her eating patterns in her journal and avoiding her feelings. She would read, and I would listen; she'd talk about what she ate, and I'd try to translate her food talk into feelings talk. When words like "hunger," "appetite," or "craving" came from Becky, they were music to my ears. Writing at her own rate and revealing and concealing what she chose, I realized, was a perfect task for a person like her. Like dieting, it kept her feeling safe and in control of her life—a disintegrating world of overstressed parents over which, in fact, she had very little control.

Through Becky's journal, I learned more about her obsessive-compulsive food rituals—how she would measure every cup of cereal and re-measure if she happened to spill a grain. I listened, continuing to speak her language of food and introduce her to my language of feelings, and as I did so, our relationship grew closer.

By the sixth week, something shifted. Becky stopped losing weight. She wasn't gaining, but her weight seemed to have hit a plateau. Her writing changed, too. Once in a while, in the middle of a typical food-obsessed journal entry, she would let slip something that showed how her worries about food and other aspects of her life were related.

> *I hate how frustrated I get in art class. I want my ideas to*
> *be perfect.*
> *Did Kelly see me blot all the oil off my pizza at lunch?*
> *Does she think I'm a nut?*

Becky closed her journal and asked me, "Do *you* think I'm a nut?" I was delighted. Instead of just reading aloud and waiting for my response, she was inviting my opinion.

"Not really a nut," I told her. "You're just someone who needs everything to be just so, to be perfect. How about writing a perfectionism list in your journal this week?" I suggested.

A week later, Becky came in with her list. It contained 22 items, from the methodical way she made her bed, tucking in the sheets in a certain order, to how she arranged her clothing closet (color coordinated), to the order that she religiously followed in doing her homework. She could not pass a mirror without checking her hair. That morning, she had blow-dried it three times.

"Wow!" I said. "You are even busier than I realized." We both laughed.

"I'm an all-or-nothing person," Becky said thoughtfully, as we explored the ways in which she ruthlessly criticized herself. Our discussions opened the door for us to look at the rigid, black-and-white thinking that limited the way she dealt with so many aspects of her life. "I'm getting to know myself better," Becky said one day. "And I think the writing is helping." So her journal, which began with a focus on food, slowly expanded and offered us a way to talk about other issues—but still not about her feelings.

In the beginning of the third month, Becky's journal provided us with a clue to the triggers that drove her to starve:

> *Tuna sandwich. I'm not going to eat it.*
> *Why can't I?*
> *When is Mom going to be home?*
> *I hate being home alone.*

"Tell me more about that," I probed. It became clear that the anxiety evoked by being home alone disappeared when Becky felt hungry. Starving and obsessing went hand in hand: When she was hungry, she couldn't stop thinking about food, and thinking about food protected her from disturbing feelings. "These moments haunt me," she said soberly. As we explored "these moments," we discovered that being home alone was the primary trigger.

This didn't surprise me. Children who feel safe and secure while growing up learn to handle a wide range of uncomfortable feelings. People in numbed-out families don't. Later in life, still yearning for the connection and intimacy they've been denied, they might abuse or restrict food to soothe themselves. I hoped that by learning to name and express her feelings with me in the office, she would be more able to sit with them when she was alone at home. For now, I hoped that writing in her journal would help with this transition.

Sure enough, Becky became aware that writing created an atmosphere of quiet thought. Simply having her journal with her, she told me, calmed her down. I was reminded of how young children use familiar items, such as teddy bears or blankets, to feel better when they are separated from the people closest to them. These transitional objects help them to feel connected while they're in day care or alone in bed at night. Perhaps Becky's journal was beginning to symbolize *our* relationship and the emotional nourishment it provided her.

One day, five months into therapy, the usually compliant Becky arrived and sat down without talking. "Is something bothering you?" I asked.

Her voice carried an edge of annoyance. "Do you think I should keep writing down what I have for breakfast every day? Isn't this boring for you?" I asked Becky if she ever thought of changing what she ate, which led to a conversation about the difficulties of changing a routine that feels so comfortable.

The next session, she came in, opened her journal, and began reading:

> *Breakfast:*
> *Cup of black coffee.*
> *Bagel without dough with veggie cream cheese.*
> *Bowl of Life with half a banana.*

At the word "Life," a huge smile spread across her face. Changing what you eat may not seem like an act of revolution to most people, but to an anorexic, it is a mystical, transformative moment that must be acknowledged. "You switched to Life?" I asked. "How did you do it?"

What surprised her was how easy it was. She wasn't sure why, but simply felt like she wanted to change. In this one small act, Becky, who had only just started to question her right/wrong, black/white thinking, moved from a position of rigidity to one of aliveness. She had opened herself up to a "Bowl of *Life*." It was an act of courage, a harbinger of growth, and a turning point.

"Doctor Rabinor, I have these voices in my head," Becky admitted at her next session. In the weeks that followed, her journal revealed an inner world inhabited by a "good" voice and a "bad" voice, which engaged in an endless squabble. Her awareness of these voices ushered in a new phase of therapy. She was beginning to realize that feeling fat was not her real problem, and her curiosity was piqued.

> *Bad Voice: If you eat all the broccoli, you can only eat two spoonfuls of noodles.*
>
> *Good Voice: You can eat all the noodles. It couldn't be more than a hundred calories.*
>
> *Bad Voice: Too much of any one thing is bad.*

"And what about feelings? I asked. "Is there a limit on how much joy or rage you can have, too?" I wanted her to reclaim her feelings, including anger at her parents, the way healthy teenagers do. In the end, I hoped that she would find a range of her own voices that expressed more than how much or how little to eat. Six weeks later she read:

> *Bad Voice: Don't decide. Let Dad decide.*
>
> *Good Voice: Dad is in a bad mood. I wish he wasn't. It's funny, when he's in a bad mood he acts just like me.*

Before Becky left that day, I wrote in the margin of her journal, "How is your dad just like you when he's in a bad mood?" When she came back for her next session, she read:

> *I always know when my dad is upset. He gets real quiet and*

doesn't talk. I feel bad for him. He's very scared. I think he feels helpless and inferior.

"Scared and helpless and inferior," I echoed. "What do you think your dad does with his feelings? How does he feel better?"

"He goes to the gym." When Becky uttered those words, I wondered if she was making the connection between her father's way and hers.

Before Becky left, we talked about how all of us take after our parents in certain ways. "It's important to understand why you are the way you are," I told her. "Then you can look at yourself in a more compassionate way—not so hard on yourself. You can tell that mean, critical voice to let up."

After reading another journal entry in which her voices struggled over the decisions she had to make, Becky looked exasperated and asked, "Why can't I *decide* about anything?"

"What's 'anything?'" She started tapping, something I had not witnessed in a while. "What's your tapping saying?" I asked. In response to her shrug, I said, "It sounds like the voices represent two parts of yourself that battle over everything, not just what you eat." She agreed. "Take a minute and just think. Perhaps something else is troubling you?"

Becky was silent for a few moments. "I have to decide where I'm sleeping this weekend. I can sleep at home even though my mom's going to be home really late, or at my Dad's on the couch."

"Making that decision must bring up a lot of feelings about your mom, your dad, and the divorce," I said. Becky looked away.

The following session she came in without a list. "That's okay," I assured her. Becky scowled. I asked, "Are you angry at me?" She said that she was not. I persevered by asking if she was getting sick of me and my instructions—make this list, make that list.

"I don't think so," she said. Tap, tap, tap. With each tap, I thought about our last session and tried to imagine what she might be feeling. I wondered, was she angry at me, afraid to tell me how she really felt, or was something else on her mind? We sat in silence. Knowing that a lot of important work gets done in the quiet, I waited a few minutes before saying, "This feels really different—what's up?"

It took her a while to spit it out. "I started writing my list, but I couldn't be bothered. I guess I did feel angry at you and fed up with your lists."

"I'm really happy you can tell me that, that you didn't hold it in." Becky looked relieved. "Are you angry at anyone else?"

After a moment's silence, she blurted out, "I'm angry at Evvie. I hate it when she doesn't give me my phone messages." That week, her stepmother had forgotten to tell Becky that her mother had called.

"What did this mean to you?" I wondered.

"I'm not important. She can't be bothered with me." And so, months after we talked about the pains in her stomach, we finally began to address the pain of divorce. Becky wrote:

> My Problems:
>
> Mom not home.
>
> Feeling unloved.
>
> When I got home today, I didn't even feel hungry but I ate a yogurt. Is that too much?
>
> I feel like I'll be doing the same rituals all my life.
>
> I feel like I don't have a father.

We spent many months exploring the various repercussions of this trauma, from how cold and empty the house had suddenly felt and how much she'd missed helping her dad work in the garden on Saturdays, to how hard it was to divide her time. By now her dad and Evvie had moved into a studio apartment in New York City. Much as she loved him, staying with him and her stepmother in such close quarters still felt uncomfortable. She was never sure whether to feel guilty for not spending enough time there or if she was in the way. "I heard Evvie tell her friend she never would have children of her own because taking care of them was too much," Becky reported sadly.

As her birthday approached, Becky started to get anxious. "Last year, I had my birthday dinner with my mom, so this year it's my dad's turn," she said. "Why does it have to be about them? It's *my* birthday, and I don't want to have it with dad and Evvie!" I encouraged Becky to ask her dad if just the two of them could have dinner together.

He agreed, but when she arrived at the restaurant, her father was there with his wife. "He said she wanted to come along and he couldn't say no and hurt her feelings. It was the worst birthday I ever had. Evvie was in a mean mood. When her fish came, she said it was too over-cooked, so my father gave her his portion. He would never do that for me," she said in a tearful voice.

Gradually, all the pain came pouring out. I listened. Once in a while, I would let Becky know that her parents' divorce was part of her—something that she would have to work on for a long time. But for now, just reconnecting with her feelings might help loosen the grip of her anorexic thoughts.

One day, Becky found a pad of paper on which her mother had itemized everything she'd bought for her in the past six months. "It really hurt me to see that! Why can't it just be normal? Why can't she just buy things for me?"

We spent some time talking about this. She told me that she remembered her mother saying, "Your father has still not paid his half of the money I've laid out for bills; if it doesn't come, you won't be able to go to sleep-away camp this summer." Becky had called her father and was stunned when he told her that he'd had some business prob-lems and might not be able to afford it and instead, maybe she should think about getting a part-time babysitting job. Although he later reneged, and she did go to camp, she was left with a sickening feeling that her needs didn't matter. From something trivial like buying a new pair of sneakers to paying for music lessons or camp, the question, "How much am I worth?" hovered like a dark storm cloud.

Knowing that financial matters can become a battleground for ex-spouses, I explained to Becky that sometimes parents' arguments about money are really about their feelings of bitterness toward each other, not the children. "But I can understand why these things make you feel unimportant and out of control of your life," I told her. "What else can't you control?"

"My frizzy hair and my zits," she replied.

"Anything else?"

"My thoughts—like the ones I have when my mother is out late."

I explained to her how people get stuck with a recurring anxious thought. "It's like a tape loop," I said. "When you're home alone, you might get a scary thought—maybe you think, 'I'm really angry at my mother. She's never here when I need her.' That thought might go around and around in your head. To protect yourself from that scary thought and the feelings behind it, your brain sends you a message: 'I feel fat.' You focus on that message instead of on your original thought because 'I feel fat' is something you can control, whereas 'I'm so angry' makes you feel like a bad, out of control person.

When you get the 'I'm fat' message, you need to recognize it as a signal that something *else* is going on. You can tell yourself, 'My programming is off. I can calm down. This is just a glitch.'" I wanted her to feel that she had some control over her thoughts, her OCD, and her eating disorder. I also wanted to emphasize that she could turn to other people when she felt lonely. "People need people," I'd remind her. "Who can you talk to?"

Soon after, she told me that her friend Cheryl had invited her to join the local choir. Becky joined, and to her surprise, loved it. Later that week, rather than stay home alone on a night when her mother was out of town on a business trip, she invited Cheryl to sleep over. This connection led to another, and she slowly began creating an intimate circle of friends. Her world began to expand, and this showed in her journal.

> *Over a year since I've been sick. Sometimes I feel better but sometimes I stand in front of the mirror for ages and look at myself and think how can I be so fat and ugly? I know that I'm not supposed to focus on these things, but I can't help it.*

> *No one knows what really bothers me, what I've been through. I still crave the attention I never got when I was little. It makes me feel so sad to think about that. All at once my life can seem to fall apart, piece by piece and suddenly, I can start to feel fat. But now, when I get that feeling, I try to fight it.*

Despite Becky's progress, the emotional weight she was carrying would occasionally trip her switch and she would find herself flirting with old ways of finding comfort, and feel ashamed for having done so.

"Take it easy on yourself," I reminded her. "Healing takes time, and obsessive thoughts are powerful foes."

By the time Becky entered her senior year of high school—two years after starting therapy—her "fat thoughts" were greatly diminished. They hadn't disappeared completely, but now we had new contexts to examine:

> *I am so insecure when it comes to my friends all being together without me. I get so jealous! And feel so disgusting! Is it depression? Nerves? Or just feelings of fatness?*

"It's easier for me to feel fat than to admit I feel mad at my dad," she volunteered one day after her father had disappointed her by not showing up to take her out for lunch.

"See what happens if, right now, you let yourself sink into how bad you felt when you realized he wasn't coming," I said. I held my breath and waited. "Let yourself be here with those memories, be with what is, as you feel everything inside." Within moments, Becky's eyes filled with tears.

In the months that followed, making room inside for her to live with her feelings of anger, abandonment, and insecurity became our mission. The words, "Just be with your feelings," became her mantra. "It helps me stay calm." Over and over, in my office, at school with her friends, and at home alone, Becky slowly learned and practiced this crucial lesson: She could, in fact, live with her feelings without resorting to calorie counting, sit ups, or starvation.

One year later, when Becky was graduating high school, her journal reflected this progress:

> *I can't think of anything except the prom. Should I have accepted the date with Rob? Or should I have waited for Chris? What if Rob stops liking me? What if Chris never calls? I go over and over this. And I feel so fat—even though I know this really isn't about being fat—just being nervous!*

Her obsession with losing weight was replaced with an "obsession" with boys. How wonderful!

Anne Frank wrote, "Paper has more patience than people." I shared the passage with Becky during one of our last sessions before she left for college, wanting her to know that her journal would always be there for her. She was still thin, but the whole team agreed that she was well enough to go. She had grown into a lively young woman—sometimes indecisive and vulnerable, but reunited with that "other" self she had described at the beginning of our work together.

In retrospect, it seems clear that out of loyalty to her family, Becky kept her feelings to herself to honor their legacy of denial and silence. While her eating disorder coincided with her parents' divorce, to say that the divorce "caused" the disorder would be an oversimplification of a complex process. Born into a family that had difficulty owning and articulating negative feelings, she was unable to digest her own.

Instead, she became preoccupied with what she believed she could control—her weight, her eating, and her body. Consciously, dieting and eating in a ritualized manner helped her lose weight; unconsciously, it anaesthetized her from the emotional trauma and tragically froze her development. Only after our relationship provided Becky with a sense of safety and security was she able to let go of her rituals that kept her grounded, yet stuck.

If symptoms are a form of forgetting, healing is based on remembering and talking. Freud taught us that. And Becky taught me that talk therapy is not simply about speaking, and journal writing is not just about writing. Therapy is about being listened to by someone who nourishes and nurtures the soul. Writing offers another kind of healing experience—a sustained self-listening. Each in their own way offered Becky a bridge to me and her inner world and helped her thaw out the frozen sea within.

8

Like Mother, Like Daughter

*Every mother contains her daughter in herself and every
daughter her mother, and every woman extends backwards
into her mother and forwards into her daughter.*
—C. J. JUNG

*A*melia was 65 years old when she entered therapy, overweight
and overwrought. When she left at the age of 69,
she was still heavier than she would have liked, but in many important
ways, she was transformed. The woman who came to my office on
Tuesdays, berating herself for her compulsive eating, apologizing for
her weight and sometimes, it seemed, for her very existence, had
become a strong, energetic person who no longer was over-involved
with food and her body.

The depth of Amelia's transformation fascinated me. Where had she found this strength? And then, not long after she left therapy, I came across an envelope she had given me as she left our final session. Inside I found a speech that Amelia's husband had written about his mother-in-law on her 90th birthday and redelivered at her funeral. Amelia must have had this speech in her possession through most of our time together, yet she had never mentioned it, nor had she told me about her mother's extraordinary accomplishments—only about her weakness, which Amelia believed she had inherited.

The speech opened up a new way of understanding Amelia, who had already surprised me many times. She reminded me that the stories we carry with us about our lives contain other, forgotten stories, and the people we believe ourselves to be are only a part of a much richer whole, just as the parents we think we know are more complicated than we realize.

Even before Amelia came to my office for her first appointment, I was struck by how courageous she was to seek therapy at her age. After all, most 65-year-olds who want to lose weight choose treatment with nutritionists, not therapists. Did she know, at some inner level, that her weight was not really the problem?

She seemed perfectly at ease as she settled into the armchair closest to mine and, with a wide smile, arranged her silver hair. Everything about this tall, strikingly attractive woman had a casual air, so her first words took me by surprise.

"I'm big, right?" She was still smiling. Unsure of how to respond, I nodded for her to continue. Instantly her eyes filled with tears.

"What just happened?" I asked.

"I'm bigger than you thought I'd be, right?" she practically whispered. I realized that Amelia had misinterpreted my nod as a confirmation of her "bigness." I'd goofed, big time. In sidestepping her question with my nod, I had confirmed her darkest fear. Later, when I had time to reflect on what had happened, I realized how much Amelia's shameful feelings about her weight haunted her; at this moment, though, I was asking myself, *How could I have been so careless?*

"I wasn't thinking about your weight," I assured Amelia. "My nod was one of welcome, my way of my asking you to tell me a little about you and your problem." My words sailed over her head.

"But I *am* big. Bigger than you thought, right?" she repeated.

"I really wasn't thinking about your size," I said, "but I see that you were. And I see you are hurt. I'm sorry that I was unintentionally hurtful."

"Don't blame yourself," she replied. "I'm the one who has the problem and has done the damage—eating, eating, eating, which is how I got this big."

With that, the story of her lifelong struggle with her body unfolded. The daughter of a large-boned mother, Amelia had been a chubby baby, a chubby child and, since her teenage years, had been locked in a pattern of dieting, bingeing, starving, and eventually bingeing again. She always regained the pounds she had lost, plus some more. She had called me, just the week before, when her weight topped 225 pounds. "That's too much, even for 5'10"," she sighed. "I'm down to 219, so I guess calling you was a good idea. Now I just have to keep it off and lose 20 more pounds, too."

Amelia was smiling again, which made me uneasy. People with eating disorders are far too willing to smile when their hearts are heavy, and to talk about their weight as a way of avoiding the issues that are "weighing them down." It was too soon to know what was really troubling Amelia, but I had already tuned in to the fact that she had a painfully poor sense of herself. First, she had reacted with feelings of shame rather than indignation when she felt criticized for her "bigness." Then, she had let me off the hook for my mistake by finding fault with herself. And now, she was downplaying the fact that she had lost six pounds in only a week.

"Six pounds is a lot of weight to take off in just a few days," I said.

And then, as if she was reading my thoughts—that crash dieting inevitably leads to starvation, starvation to overeating, and overeating to more weight gain—she said, "But the problem isn't losing it. It's keeping it off. My downfall is snacking."

Just the previous weekend, Rick, her husband of 45 years, had come into the kitchen while she was nibbling her way through a cake. "Your eating is out of control," he growled in a tone that chilled her to the core. He was right, Amelia shamefully acknowledged, for she was eating more than ever. Usually his criticism caused her to withdraw, she told me, but this time, she surprised herself by fighting back. She yelled, he yelled, and finally, in a moment of exasperation, Rick suggested that Amelia find a therapist. To her own surprise, Amelia agreed.

"But now that I'm here, where do I begin?"

I asked Amelia to close her eyes and go back in her mind to the moment when she was eating the cake. "Take a moment and remember what was happening and what you were feeling about the cake." Within seconds, she opened her eyes.

"I am sitting in the kitchen and have just finished talking on the telephone to my daughter, Lynda."

Letting the image sink in for a few moments, I finally asked, "What were you talking about?"

"Not much," she replied, which was a phrase I would hear many times from Amelia. "We were talking about my mother. Her name is Mary, but we call her 'Grammy.'" As I discovered with some more prompting, she and her daughter had been arguing about who would take care of Grammy that day. Who would take her to the doctor, the supermarket, the hairdresser?

"I'm missing something," I said. "What's happened to your mother?" Only a month earlier, Amelia's mother had been diagnosed with Alzheimer's. The problem had been brewing for some time, but until the diagnosis, the whole family had ignored the signs. After living alone for almost 50 years since the death of her husband, Grammy was now increasingly incapable of doing anything for herself. She had recently moved in with Lynda, who lived nearby. Since then, Lynda and Amelia spoke many times a day, and their conversations usually ended on a resentful note.

"My daughter is really angry at me," Amelia said. "She keeps saying, 'Ma, she's your mother. Don't leave me with all the responsibility.' But the truth is, I wanted to find a nursing home for Grammy, and Lynda adamantly refused." Just as her voice was developing a hard edge, Amelia smiled and changed the subject. "But that's not why I'm here," she said lightly. "My mother is not the real problem. I'm here because of my weight."

Clearly, Amelia was comfortable talking about her life and herself on the most superficial level, but as soon as the subject started to get more intimate, she retreated. Wanting to avoid a dialogue about weight, I asked about her immediate family. She happily complied, proudly telling me that she had raised two daughters, had a wonderful husband who recently had handed over the reigns of the consulting firm he had built to a younger associate, and that they shared a good life. Then, without shifting her voice a decibel, she jumped back to the subject of her mother.

"Grammy can no longer get around or manage her everyday life the way she could only a few months ago." Not only was Grammy's life radically altered, so was Amelia's. Her days were consumed with her mother's errands. "My time," she admitted, "is packed, if not overflowing, with my mother's chores." As she spoke, her eyes narrowed and her face grew dark. "She could keep me busy from morning till night, writing checks, arranging her food cabinets, even tying her shoelaces. But I'm boring you." And Amelia's smile returned.

A professor of mine once said that the clues to every patient's problem are hidden in the first session. After Amelia left, I asked myself what themes had emerged. I thought about her smile. Was it masking anxiety or shame? Most people have both feelings on first seeing a therapist. Her initial comments were all about her outside, her size, her "bigness." Was this because she felt empty inside?

Here was a woman who belittled herself and invited others to criticize her. She also minimized her feelings. I thought about how sad, scared, and burdened I would feel if my mother was spiraling down the path of Alzheimer's. Except for the two moments when she let slip some resentment, Amelia had reported on her mother's deterioration with a mildness that confused me. Perhaps she did not want me to see how annoyed she felt about having to care for her. Did she feel guilty? Or was she compelled to present herself in a way that she thought would please me?

I kept coming back to her smile. I sensed a little, longing voice behind it calling out, "Please like me. I'll be what *you* want me to be: agreeable, compliant, and pleasant." Her smile made me think about what we call a "false self," which has no agenda beyond pleasing others. It appears to be well-adjusted, but in fact, the false self is a wounded self. It develops as a defense against the fear of being told that we are wrong, bad, not good enough, that our feelings aren't real and our voices don't count. It forms in our very first relationship, the relationship with our mother.

From the beginning, working with Amelia was unique in many ways. First, there was her age. When I work with teenagers, I am always brought back to my own adolescence, whereas Amelia put me in touch with the years of my life that were around the corner. Second, even though she was in pain, she didn't have a life-threatening condition, as do many of my bulimic and anorexic patients; I didn't feel the pressure to move her out of a danger zone as fast as possible. I could focus instead on creating an atmosphere of quiet thought where she could begin to make sense of her symptoms.

With no treatment team to coordinate, I felt more relaxed than usual. I could simply listen to Amelia to draw her out and learn more about her. As I anticipated, she turned out to be a bright, talkative woman who welcomed insight and quickly developed self-understanding. In fact, by the end of our second session she let me know that she suspected there was an emotional component to her eating. However, the session opened with Amelia doing what many compulsive eaters do: blaming her weight on her biology.

"I think my metabolism has come to a halt," she said as she settled into a seat in my office. Although it's seldom the whole story, biology *can* be a factor in weight problems, especially in someone who has been chubby since childhood, so I was certainly not going to dismiss her theory outright. Besides, I wanted Amelia to start separating her feelings about the way she looked from the way she felt about how she ate, and to start looking at the issues underlying her eating.

"We're not all meant to be 150 pounds at 5'10", I told her. "We only think so because our culture is prejudiced about size. But there are many reasons why some people can't lose weight or keep off the weight they've lost." I went on to explain that we are still in the early stages of understanding how brain chemicals and metabolism affect binge eating and body size. In addition to all the emotional factors, there are numerous physical reasons why some people can't lose weight, such as medications that affect appetite and hormone levels, and differing caloric needs. According to one theory, everyone has a self-regulating mechanism called a set point that helps the body keep its fat stores at a certain level. Everybody's set point is different. When your fat stores fall below the level your body has set, your system goes to work by increasing your appetite and slowing down your metabolism so that you'll regain whatever fat you've lost.

"In any case," I continued, "that's what we're here to figure out—how much of the problem is biological and how much has to do with your eating habits, which could be a reflection of something deeper. We have to look at everything that's going on and try to tease out the threads."

Amelia was silent for a moment before she told me, sheepishly, that there was another reason she had gone along with her daughter's suggestion that she see a therapist. She recently had read a letter in the advice column of a local paper from an overweight woman whose husband constantly interrupted her. In her letter, the woman wondered if her eating problem and her husband's seeming lack of respect might be connected. Something had clicked in Amelia's mind.

"Don't get me wrong," she said. "Basically, Rick and I get along beautifully. We share a lot of interests—books, opera, music. We have a good life, and he's been a wonderful husband. Unlike me, he's a dynamo, very youthful and funny, but sometimes at my expense."

"How, at your expense?" I asked.

"He can be demeaning. He interrupts me a lot, like cutting in while I'm on the phone to offer me bits of advice. And when I try to tell him about something, he has a habit of stopping me short by walking away or starting to opening his mail while I'm talking. I'm sure he doesn't mean to be so disrespectful, but . . . "

"How do you handle it?"

"I try to point it out, but he's had a series of heart attacks. And anyway, Rick's not the only one who interrupts. My children do it all the time and always have. I suppose they learned it from him. It makes me angry, but it annoys me even more that I can't seem to do anything about it," she added without a trace of anger.

When I asked her what she did with her angry feelings, Amelia smiled wanly. "I guess I just feel annoyed." She was used to feeling irked and not telling anyone. "People have always had a hard time reading me," she said. "Rick used to tell the kids, 'Look out for your mom. She can say and act like everything is fine and then suddenly, all hell can break loose.'" But when I asked Amelia to tell me about "all hell," she laughed. "He exaggerated. I rarely lose it." This was a point we returned to repeatedly in the first few months.

"How did you learn to 'rarely lose it'? From your mother? Your father?" I asked her.

"I never thought about it," Amelia replied, using another phrase that I would soon come to associate with her.

A couple of sessions later, she told me a story that helped me to better understand. She had grown up with a quiet father and a "dopey" mother who sought comfort from Amelia rather than offering it. When Amelia was about seven, Grammy had become involved in a terrible fight with her own mother and had come to Amelia for solace. "I remember her crying on my shoulder. I felt so sorry for her, but I didn't know how to help." I asked Amelia to think about what that was like; her answer was telling. "I know now that my mother shouldn't have burdened me, but that's just how it was. You know, my mother always used to say, 'When the world gives you a lemon, make lemonade.'"

My picture of Amelia was getting clearer still. I guessed that she had been "making lemonade" all her life, instead of voicing her complaints and desires. She had such a long history of thinking that she had no right to speak and be heard that, by now, she had no voice left. Perhaps she was afraid of rocking the boat by asserting herself, as if doing so might expose a part of her that she had banished. Maybe she didn't value herself enough to imagine that she could still be loved if she stood up to others. One thing was certain: Amelia needed to become more comfortable with her negative feelings.

For now, I would have to listen vigilantly and stay alert to her moods, especially to any signs of annoyance at me. I hoped that by doing so, I would be able to let her know that these feelings are normal in every relationship. It was also important to let her know that I took her and her feelings seriously. Until she developed a level of comfort with confrontation, I would have to be very careful about interrupting her.

After a few months of treatment, Amelia reported feeling more comfortable with her eating, and so we turned our attention to the rest of her life. She had little sense of pride, just as she had little sense of outrage. She would minimize her strengths, adding the words, "I haven't done *that* much" or "I never really thought about it. I just did what I had to do," to her story of raising Lynda, while helping her husband build a business.

Amelia told me early on that she was an avid watercolorist. I asked her to bring in some of her paintings, and when she finally did, I was amazed by her artistic talent. After much prodding about her techniques, I finally asked, "Have you ever thought of framing these?" The paintings obviously had been lying in a pile in some drawer at home.

Meanwhile, she reported dispassionately on her mother's deterioration and the family's struggles to cope. I listened with all my heart and constantly let Amelia know how much I empathized with her, by assuring her that she was faced with a situation that was both tragic and burdensome. By filling in the emotional side of her story, I hoped that I would help Amelia take all her complicated feelings surrounding Grammy's illness seriously and understand that feeling torn up because your mother has Alzheimer's is normal. It is a heavy load, fraught with worries like, "How long will this go on? Am I going to get it, too?"

One day, when we were exploring the triggers that drove her to nibble, Amelia told me that she had noticed a pattern: Her overeating seemed to be connected to being at home. "I don't know why that should be," she said. "A lot of people would be thrilled to have the life I have."

She had just been describing yet another resentful phone conversation with Lynda about who would take Grammy to the doctor.

"I think that, by stuffing your mouth with food, you stop yourself from confronting Lynda with the fact that she's the one who insisted on your mother not being cared for in a home," I ventured. It was also becoming clear that Amelia wanted to avoid the agony of her mother's deterioration and Amelia's guilt about the fact that her daughter had taken her in. So, instead, she would eat and say, "I'm a bad person for eating," rather than, "I'm a bad person for not wanting to take care of my mother."

However, Grammy's worsening condition was only part of the story. "Lynda *loves* her grandmother so," Amelia told me. "In fact, she seems to love her more than she loves me!" She was astounded, she said, because she herself could never get along with Grammy.

"All of us miss out on some things during our childhood," I said. "I'm wondering about you and Grammy. What kind of mother was she?"

"Why talk about the past?" she responded. "I was a chubby girl, that's all I remember. And my mother hated my chubbiness. What else? Who remembers?"

"We talk about the past," I said, "because it plays itself out in the present. You might be 65 years old and think it doesn't matter any more, but it does."

As it turned out, Amelia did remember. She had been the only daughter of four children, and the least favored. Since childhood, she had lived with the sense of being misunderstood and unimportant. "My mother never really liked me," she said. Grammy herself had grown up in dire poverty and had made an ethic out of austerity, both material and emotional. Amelia, I came to realize, was something of a motherless child who, like so many of my patients, had learned to soothe herself and compensate with food. I felt for her as she spoke of her barren childhood, and of "sitting on the edge of my bed in our apartment in Brooklyn looking out over the rooftops, wondering what would become of me."

People who have never given themselves the time or permission to talk about their lives learn a lot just from listening to themselves tell their stories. In telling hers to me, Amelia began to realize that she had a reason to feel angry, and to understand why she did not want to care for her mother. None of her "special brothers" were involved with Grammy's care now. Amelia was the one who had to "babysit" a mother who, she felt, had never cared for her.

Amelia started to experience grief, too. She was surprised at her sense of loss for a mother "who was never really there much anyway." She tried to push these feelings away by saying, "We were never close." Her descriptions of her childhood helped me to understand why, even now, she could not care enough about herself to make anything seem worth fighting for.

At the same time, another mystery began to unravel. I had been puzzled by Amelia's sense of herself as boring, because I found her anything but. She led an interesting, full life, she attended cultural events with her husband, and she was an accomplished artist. Yet she would often say, "Am I boring you?" She could be talking about an opera or visits from her kids, when suddenly she would stop herself mid-sentence to ask if I was really interested in what she was saying.

And then, one day, she told me, "Of all the people I have ever known in my life, my mother was the saddest. She was like a rag doll, always down, indecisive and shy. I'd have to get involved in all sorts of things, even what flavor ice cream she wanted. She had a horrible life," Amelia said, describing the emotional and financial poverty of her mother's childhood and adulthood. "She would always tell me how lucky I was. Her own mother hated her and, one day when she was being disobedient, hit her on the head with a frying pan. She's been partially deaf ever since."

I instantly recognized in Amelia's description of her mother the woman that Amelia thought *she* was: a victim. I thought about the powerful legacies passed down from mother to daughter, and everything began to make more sense. Amelia identified herself as boring and depressed because she identified with her boring and depressed mother; she felt that she was just like her.

It might seem strange for a woman to feel so linked to a mother she describes as "not being there," but that is far from unusual. When a person grows up longing for love or recognition from an unresponsive parent, they feel, as a child, that their best chance at getting what they need is by being just like that parent. Even as an adult, they never feel free to become their own person.

Amelia's compliance made more sense, too. Here she was, avoiding conflict with a husband who demeaned her and a daughter who bullied her, denying feelings that boiled up inside, numbing herself with food, and then feeling angry at herself for her "bad habit." How interesting, I thought, that she had grown up with a mother who had been severely punished for speaking out. Amelia had learned to dance to another's drummer. She had learned to stay in line and use food to compensate for her lack of a true self.

As Amelia told her story, I also found myself wondering to what extent Grammy's deafness had contributed to her sense of not being heard as a child. I thought about how easy it would be for a mother to tune out because she could neither hear the front door slam when her children came home from school nor their bickering when they were playing upstairs.

"What a horrible story," I said, hoping to breathe some of my empathy for both mother and daughter into Amelia.

We are used to the idea that pent-up hostility is dangerous, but pent-up love is another real tragedy. We all want to love our parents, and feel better about ourselves when we are free to show it. On the other hand, when we see them as inadequate, we see ourselves in the same way.

I wanted Amelia to feel more like a survivor than a victim, strong instead of passive and powerless. Amelia the victim let herself be bulldozed; if she could start by confronting her daughter over the issue of Grammy's care, she might experience her own power. So, one day when she was "making lemonade" out of Lynda's accusations that she was shirking her responsibilities, I suggested, "Why don't you take a moment to think about what you *really* want to say to your daughter?"

She sat there for a few moments and finally said in a weak voice, "I want her to know that I don't want to give up every Sunday to babysit Grammy."

"Tell her more," I encouraged. "Imagine Lynda sitting in that chair. Tell her exactly how you feel."

"Lynda, Grammy should be in a senior day-care program every day from 8 A.M. to 5 P.M."

"Is there more?"

"Lynda, this is too much for you. You work long hours and need some time to be out with your friends. You're too young to have such a restricted life."

"What does Lynda say?"

"I don't know. I think she knows I'm right. We need help."

By involving her in this type of role-play, I helped Amelia rehearse a more assertive role. Soon, she started to grapple with real problems, rather than be a victim of her mother and daughter. With my support, she researched day care for her mother and, within a couple of months, had found a center and talked her daughter into the idea.

Amelia also started tell her husband what she wanted instead of always going along with his wishes. Little by little, her wishes and ideas were becoming more important to her. She discovered that she would not upset the apple cart if, for instance, she went into her studio to paint rather than watch the World Series with her husband, as he expected her to do. And little by little, her weight began to drop.

Nothing could have prepared me for what happened next. I was waiting for Amelia one Tuesday in October and 1:15 came and went. No Amelia. This was unusual; after six months I knew that she prided herself on being punctual. After 10 more minutes had passed, I called her home. There was no answer, and no answering machine, either. I tidied up my office, watered my plants, and then glanced at the session notes from our last meeting, but no clues emerged.

By noon the next day, Amelia had neither called nor come in, but later that afternoon, when I checked my machine, her familiar, soft voice greeted me. "It's Amelia. I know we had an appointment yesterday, but something happened. If you have any time tomorrow, I'll come in and…I guess I'll explain it all then."

The following day, I found her sitting in my waiting room with her eyes closed. Usually she got up as she heard me coming, but this time she just sat there. "Are you okay?" I asked. She shook her head. It was only after she had made herself comfortable in my office that she said, "You'll never believe this one." Once she began talking, she didn't stop until she had told me every detail of the past 72 hours, beginning with the arrival of her oldest childhood friend, Roslyn, who had flown in from Pittsburgh on Monday to stay overnight before catching a flight for the Orient. Amelia detailed the history of their forty-year friendship, the problems they'd had at the airport, and exactly what they had eaten for dinner. Afterward, Amelia settled her friend in the guestroom. "Rick and I were watching TV, and suddenly she burst into the room, screaming, 'Someone help me!'" They all ran into the guestroom. Flames were everywhere. By the time fire engines arrived, the fire had traveled through two-thirds of the house.

"I guess I was the sanest," Amelia told me as she recalled finding herself in the street, watching the home she had lived in for two decades burn almost to the ground, while Rick stood frozen in panic and Roslyn wailed hysterically about her baggage, her trip, her plane tickets.

As Amelia told her story, I tried to imagine the scene: four trucks, a forest of ladders, firemen invading her house room by room; black smoke and the deafening groans and explosions as the roof caved in and the house collapsed; 28 years of photos, letters, paintings reduced to wisps of black and gray smoke and ash. I was astounded by her calm in the face of what had happened, as if the process of telling the tale was having an almost hypnotic effect.

Most of us unconsciously believe that we'll never be struck by the catastrophes that befall others. We tell ourselves, "It can't happen to me." When reality intervenes, as it did for Amelia, we suddenly come face-to-face with our vulnerability, even our mortality. In the weeks following Amelia's fire I waited for her to react to the enormity of this loss. But, to my surprise, Amelia did not collapse under the weight. Although she made a ritual of recalling the events of those 72 hours, she talked just as much about the progress she was making in having the house renovated. She took charge of everything, from hiring contractors to dealing with auditors and wading through the remains of her home, repairing or replacing what she could. Just listening to all that Amelia had to contend with exhausted me. But none of it seemed to exhaust Amelia; on the contrary, she found her life exhilarating. And with it, she stopped nibbling, and her weight dropped rapidly. By December, she was able to tell me, "I didn't have an eating disorder. I ate because I was depressed. The fire empowered me."

Amelia was both right and wrong. She was depressed, but she also had an eating disorder. People eat to medicate themselves for a host of problems, depression being one of them. But this wasn't the time for me to challenge her. I simply rejoiced with her.

As the weeks went by, however, I asked myself, "How is she doing this?" She seemed to have tapped into an underground spring of energy and resiliency. What in her life had prepared her for this? I knew that, at an early age, Amelia had learned to cope with what life handed her—to make lemonade out of lemons. In this particular case, the lesson served her well. Dealing with the aftermath of the fire also gave her a vacation from caring for, and thinking about, her mother. She was relieved to be freed from that responsibility. Nevertheless, I was still intrigued by her transformation. It was not until later, in reading her husband's account of Grammy's life, that I would fully grasp the source and significance of Amelia's awakening.

Armed with her new sense of power, she began to assert herself for the first time in her life. One day, she told me that, quite by chance, she had discovered some sketchpads lying in the dumpster that had become a permanent fixture outside her house. With an indignation that I had not heard in her voice before, she said, "I pulled them out and there they were—pads from years ago into which I had poured my heart and soul. How had they gotten into the trash? I stormed back inside and—this is very unlike me, you know—I said, 'Rick.' I must have sounded different, because usually it's hard to get his attention when he's watching TV, but this time he looked up. I had those soggy sketchpads in my hands. '*Why were these in the dumpster?*'

"He tried to make light of it, but I wouldn't let him wiggle out. This time I just wouldn't. I told him that those sketchpads were *mine* to keep, throw away, or do with whatever I chose. I made sure he heard. 'Mine, do you understand?' I repeated. 'It's not for you to throw away my things— never, never . . . ' " Amelia paused. "I was *so* angry. Angry isn't even the word, Judy. I was outraged! Finally, after all sorts of arguments from him about the charred and waterlogged remains of all of our stuff that we have to go through, I got him to promise me that he would not touch any of my things ever again."

I was delighted. While I was far from sure that Amelia's transformation was permanent, I knew that every time we stand up for ourselves as she had just done, we strengthen that pathway inside of us.

A couple of weeks later, I went for a walk on the beach with a friend. Climbing over the dunes at the end of my street, I took in the rich smell of the ocean and the seagulls' cries. The beach was deserted, save for two middle-aged women who stood thigh-high in the quiet sea, bundled in fishing gear. After our walk, the image of the fisherwomen stayed with me, and I recalled a saying that I love: Give a man a fish and he has food for a day; give him a fishing rod and he has food for a lifetime.

Those words made me think of Amelia. During her first six months of therapy she had picked up, tentatively at first, the rod that I offered her—the sense of herself as a competent person who had every right to make her wishes heard, and, in fact, owed it to herself to do so. In the wake of the fire she had grabbed that rod and used it to nourish herself in the best way possible.

In December, Amelia came in for her last session before leaving with Rick for Florida, where they spent three months in the wintertime. She was dressed in a black velvet outfit for an evening at the ballet. "I've lost 34 pounds," she said proudly. "I've not only taken them off, I've kept them off."

"You look like you *feel* like a million dollars!" I said, emphasizing that her new look was a reflection of the new person she was on the inside. I wanted Amelia to bask in the sunshine of not only the weight loss, but also the emotional work behind it, so I asked, "What do you think helped?" As we reviewed the past several months, she returned to the fire as the catalyst that had changed her life.

"Things feel very different in the room this session," I commented. "You seem almost reborn." She beamed.

"You mean that I am different," she said, "that this fire—this tragedy—offered me the opportunity to find myself." And with this statement, Amelia began to recall the baby steps of her growth. When she had first come to see me, she was adrift, with no sense of purpose. Her husband had retired; days that had been hers to shape as she chose suddenly became "his." Doing menial chores while Rick kept himself busy in his home office made her feel inconsequential, and his constant nagging made it worse. The fire had changed all of that.

"People think that once we reach adulthood, we stop growing," I mused, "but your story shows that each life stage comes with new opportunities. You've had to deal with your mother's Alzheimer's, your husband's retirement, and your changing body. That's a lot. Every one of these things has meant a shift in your relationships with the people closest to you, including yourself. Maybe you weren't prepared to make those shifts."

Amelia smiled and then said wistfully, "You know, I might not need to see you any more after I get back from Florida. I feel so much better, and my eating problem has improved no end."

But Amelia's treatment was far from over. Several days after her return from Florida, she called to make an appointment. When she came in, her first words were, "She's not dead, but the mother I knew is gone." Both Amelia and Lynda had been at the hospital the entire weekend after Grammy slipped into a Sundown State, a tragic stage of Alzheimer's disease. She had been rushed to the hospital after being found wandering the streets, naked.

We spent the session talking about how heartbreaking it was to watch her mother deteriorate. Only as Amelia was getting up to leave did she say, "You know, I didn't get to tell you today, but this weekend my eating was out of control again. I spent two whole days eating."

"There are worse things than eating when our suffering is too much to bear, when our hearts are broken," I said, hoping to help her be less self-critical and have more empathy for herself.

"And another thing. I've had this terrible pain," she continued, putting her hand over her stomach. "All weekend long, I've had a burning sensation right here, and I understand something now: The pain is connected to my eating. Maybe I eat because of that pain. Is it possible that I eat to make that pain go away?" We both smiled.

"It's possible," I said. She grew quiet and so I prodded, "Does it work? Does the eating help the pain go away?" I wanted to make her aware that she was eating for a reason, albeit a harmful one.

"Maybe I have an ulcer," she said, and I felt as if she were a bumble-bee, about to light on one flower, then suddenly flitting off to another.

"Do *you* think it's an ulcer?" I asked, and, once again, we both laughed. "I think we have spent the session talking about how heart-breaking it is to see your mother deteriorate," I added, "and the pain in your stomach is your body telling you just that."

"I think I eat because of that pain, to soothe that feeling. I feel like there's a burning in my stomach." She paused. "There *are* ulcers in my family."

Before Amelia left, I suggested that she see a medical doctor to rule out a gastric problem, and I taught her a simple visualization exercise that I hoped would help her get in touch with the place where her mind and her body connected. People tend to avoid pain; I wanted Amelia to let herself go into it and realize that it would not break her.

Amelia did not return the following week, or the next, because her mother had died shortly after our last session. When she finally did come in, she was more agitated than I'd expected. "Lynda dropped a bomb on me the night before the funeral," she began. "She told me the reason Grammy had lived with her was because Grammy had made her promise never to let her wind up in an old-age home." This secret pact greatly distressed Amelia, who felt ashamed that her mother hadn't asked *her*. In Amelia's mind, Grammy must have known that she wouldn't make or keep such a promise, even though it was the family tradition to "take care of one's own." In fact, Grammy took in her own mother, whom she hated, when she was dying, and Amelia had taken in her father before he died. Amelia was torn: Should she have done the same for Grammy?

It was only at the very end of our session that Amelia brought up the issue of food. "I've slipped into my old pattern of snacking," she said. I tried to reassure her that reverting to her old habit in the face of losing her mother and learning about "the pact" was perfectly understandable. Certainly, there are worse things than overeating, I repeated. Yet, as I listened to her, I was troubled by the shame that she continued to feel, especially after all the work we had done together over two-and-a-half years. A little voice kept nagging at me: *Is there something else at the heart of her bingeing that neither of us knows about?* I'd thought that the fire had led to Amelia's breakthrough, but by now it was clear that there could be more to learn.

Before Amelia left, I told her about a new technique I had recently started practicing that has helped patients overcome lifetime struggles with addictions, obsessions, depression, and eating disorders. About a year earlier, I'd met an old friend and colleague for lunch who told me that she had been trained in this new psychotherapy approach, called Eye Movement Desensitization Reprocessing (EMDR), and that it had changed her practice. It involved integrating different forms of rhythmical brain stimulation, such as eye movements and hand taps or sonic tones, into conventional talk therapy in a way that seemed to help patients deal with painful past experiences. My friend told me that EMDR had helped many of her stuck patients to "jump-start" the healing process. What's more, their success had come relatively quickly.

Initially, I was filled with mixed feelings: skepticism, enthusiasm, curiosity. I couldn't fully understand what she was describing, but her enthusiasm was inspiring. It made me feel hopeful for the many people with eating disorders who, like Amelia, cannot completely resolve their food issues no matter how much therapy they do or how many methods they try. My friend was so persuasive that, at her suggestion, I signed up for a training course.

EMDR is based on the natural workings of the body. It was invented by Francine Shapiro, Ph.D., who noticed that when she moved her eyes back and forth, painful memories became less powerful. She hypothesized that eye movements and other kinds of bilateral stimulation activate a healing process that helps a person bring all the resources of her conscious mind to heal the wounded part of herself.

Nobody is sure exactly how or why rapid eye movements help a person to process or reprocess experiences, but scientists theorize that properly processed memories "live" in both sides of the brain, while raw, unprocessed, traumatic memories are lodged in only one side. The rhythmical stimulation of EMDR helps connect the two sides of the brain. My personal experience was that during the training course, when we practiced EMDR on each other, a terrifying memory that had plagued me since childhood became benign and my feelings about it completely transformed.

By the time the weekend was over, I had made a decision to both work on myself with a private EMDR therapist and continue training. And when Amelia came in after the funeral, still stuck in her old feelings about herself, I felt ready to try this new technique with her. During her next session, I explained how it worked, and asked if she would think about giving it a try. When she came back the following week, she was willing and ready.

"My eating has been out of control the past few days," she told me. She had woken up that morning with a terrible backache. "I went into the kitchen to get some ice packs, and the next thing I knew, I was in bed lying on them, watching TV and stuffing peanuts in my mouth." The more she talked, the more she seemed to feel disgusted with herself. I reminded her that we both knew it wasn't really the peanuts she was hungry for, and suggested trying the EMDR. She agreed, and I explained that we would be following a specific set of procedures designed to maximize healing.

"To begin," I said, "see if you can bring up the most distressing part of the memory." Amelia pictured herself in bed at 7 A.M. gobbling peanuts. I asked her to look at that image and describe a negative belief about herself, followed by a positive self-statement that she would rather believe. Amelia said that she felt "out of control" and would like to feel "in control." When I asked her what emotions and physical sensations she experienced with her image, she listed self-disgust, along with a pounding in her chest and weakness in her legs. Amelia rated her distress around that image as intense, at a level ten on a scale of one to ten.

I asked her to stay with the images of lying in bed and the feelings, negative beliefs, and bodily sensations and to follow with her eyes the rhythm of my fingers as they moved back and forth across her field of vision. She was amazed by how quickly new images flooded her mind. The first was of her brother, Alan, who was depressed, sneaky, weak-willed, and always got the chocolates he whined for.

"Go with that," I said.

"I didn't have treats and I was always hungry. We didn't have much money to buy things. On holidays we always had peach pies because we had a peach tree in our yard."

"Stay with that."

"I used to take pennies . . . later on I found out they needed them. My mother saved pennies, but I didn't know that. I felt hungry…I bought so many goodies with those pennies— jelly beans, chocolates, and those dots of colored sugar on long strips of paper—do you re-member them?" I did. "They gave me so much pleasure."

"Go with that," I repeated.

"I begin with a handful of pennies and keep going back into the kitchen to get more. I take a dozen at a time and think that's smart, but it isn't. It's a dumb thing, but I do it anyway, and I dislike myself …I take the pennies. She saved pennies."

I was amazed. Amelia was bringing up something new from her childhood that spoke volumes about how her sense of shame was linked with her guilt over eating and wanting. Not only was she ashamed as a little girl because her mother didn't like her, she was ashamed because she was sneaking pennies to buy the kinds of treats given to her brothers.

When I later asked her whether she had ever thought about this aspect of her past while we were working together, she said, "I guess I never really paid it much attention. But now I see. There was never enough—money or candy or anything."

"That session really made me think," Amelia remarked when she came in the next time. "I've been going over it all week. During the EMDR, I kept getting to deeper levels, and I realized I was eating when I wasn't hungry. It's like the pennies. I say I want something, and now I see that feeling has been with me forever—wanting something and feeling ashamed for wanting it."

"What did you want?" I asked.

Amelia's eyes filled. "I guess I wanted to be wanted," she said sadly. After a pause, she continued, "If they didn't want to have me, why did they? I was their only girl, but I always had the feeling my mother didn't care about me. I was the least favorite."

Although Amelia and I had discussed this many times, she was now able to make a completely new connection between wanting something and being unwanted. Even more important was her expanded perspective on her relationship with her mother. Instead of feeling guilty and believing that *she* was at fault, she wondered, "What was wrong with *Grammy* that she gave the boys so much more?"

For the first time since I had known her, Amelia seemed truly angry with her mother. I remembered how, after the fire, she had let herself feel and express her anger toward her husband; even then, the most she could muster for her mother was resentment and a gnawing recognition of having been cheated. Now I could see that she was *experiencing* what previously she had only known intellectually. The anger filled her body, flushed her face, and made her voice strong.

"Last time, I really felt what it was like to be that little girl, and thinking about it the past few days, I just feel so mad. It makes me furious, as a mother myself, to think that my own mother could be so harsh, so uncaring." This was an entirely different Amelia than the one who had complained about having to babysit Grammy. Her anger was woven with compassion for herself. She also felt protective towards the child that she had been.

We tend to fear anger as a "negative" emotion, but it can be transformative. Anger energizes because, unlike resignation or resentment, it implies hope and expectations—"I deserved better and life can be better." For Amelia, feeling angry to the core allowed her to be her true self instead of the false one that dismissed her feelings about a mother who didn't love her enough, a husband who didn't respect her, and a daughter whom she feared hated her. Compassion for herself translated into compassion for Grammy, who, she finally realized, had done the best that she could, given *her* history. This was a big step. People are afraid to acknowledge their mother's pain, fearing that if they feel sorry for her, they will no longer be entitled to their own injured feelings. But Amelia had come to realize that she could feel sorry for the poverty of her mother's life and still feel angry with her. With this, she expanded internally.

Not long after her EMDR session, Amelia came in, bouncing with a real lightness of spirit that contrasted sharply with the assumed breeziness of our early sessions. "Judy, I have something to tell you," she said. "I had lunch with Lynda a couple of days ago—she invited me—and I feel as if a weight has lifted off my shoulders."

Lynda had confided in her mother during their lunch together. "That in itself surprised me no end," Amelia told me. But what Lynda wanted her to know was even more surprising. She had decided to have a baby, even though she was unmarried, and was already looking for a sperm donor. Although Amelia's initial response was shock, she didn't react, but let Lynda just talk. She took in her daughter's reality—that at age 40, it was now or never—and empathized with her.

Then she went home and explained to her husband Lynda's decision to become a "single mother by choice," rather than allow him to label her an "unwed mother." By supporting her daughter, Amelia broke the cycle of neglect and disconnection that had persisted in her family for three generations.

"What's more," she said, "I realized that I've been so focused on how bad I felt about Lynda promising to take care of Grammy, instead of putting her in an assisted living facility, I never thought about how it must have felt for Lynda to *keep* that promise. When I asked her, she told me it was a nightmare. She couldn't say no because she had no idea what it would really mean to have someone with Alzheimer's living with her." Understanding her daughter's experience helped Amelia to connect with her in an entirely new way.

Before she left, I asked Amelia to bring up and rate the original distressing image of lying in bed eating peanuts. It had diminished in intensity and was down from a ten to a one. Of course, Amelia's transformation was about much more than peanuts. It was as if all at once she was set free from the sources of her shameful problem. What had freed her was her new ability to first feel anger about, and then grieve her early losses, which in turn allowed her to live more fully in the present. Instead of reliving the past through her eating disorder, Amelia found the nourishment she had been longing for in her new, more open relationship with her daughter.

I only saw Amelia a few more times before she said she no longer wanted to continue therapy. Although she still sometimes snacked when she wasn't hungry, she no longer ate automatically; and when she did snack, she no longer felt ashamed about it. "No one is in control all the time," she said during our last session. "And I'm not so concerned with my weight anymore. I guess I've really grown."

Two months later, the final piece of Amelia's puzzle fit into place: Where had she found the inner strength to rebuild her house after the fire, which was the first step in her transformation? I was organizing my files, and came across the manila envelope that Amelia had handed me as she left my office for the last time. Stretched to the limit by life's demands, I had forgotten about it. Curious, I began to read.

I learned about Grammy's desolate childhood on a poor Irish farm, her journey to America alone at age 17, her early days in a new country working 29 days a month for $35, her marriage, motherhood, and the family's struggles to make ends meet during the depression. It was a portrait of a woman who had triumphed over hardship, whose powerful determination and resiliency had been the salvation of her family. I was stunned. This was not the sad, dependent mother whom Amelia had described to me in the course of three years of treatment.

And then I read a passage that made me catch my breath. *"One night in her dream Grammy received her answer: Build a house on the back of the property and rent out the main house."* And so, for months, Grammy raided demolition sites for scrap lumber and building supplies and organized Amelia and her brothers in the project of refurbishing them. Amelia straightened nails while her brothers cleared the land and lugged heavier materials. Grammy sought out blueprints, designed additions, dealt with the Buildings Department and, together with family and friends, set to work building. "Thus, with the fortitude of Ma Joad, the Grace of God, and the indomitable grit and courage of Grammy, the family survived the Great Depression."

Those words stopped me in my tracks. I immediately remembered the fire. So this is where Amelia had found the strength and enthusiasm to cope with a crisis that would leave most people feeling thoroughly hopeless. I thought about how often we find buried parts of ourselves when we're dropped off at the end of the train track. Beyond this, I realized that after the fire, Amelia must have tapped into a lost memory of her mother as the strong survivor that she was.

For most of her life, Amelia could only see the aspects of her mother that were distressing to her as a child—the sad image of Grammy that had shaped Amelia's sense of herself. In telling her story again here, though, I find myself wondering whether the EMDR, which helped her to feel compassion for herself as a child and an adult, also opened her up to a more compassionate and complex view of her mother, one that included both weakness and strength, sadness and determination. Was that how Amelia finally found the "grit and courage" in herself?

One summer, I returned from a trip to Russia with an exquisite, wooden, hand-painted doll. Only a few inches high, the doll looks simple, yet things are never what they seem to be. The doll can be unscrewed, and within it is a smaller doll, and a smaller one within that, and so on. There are seven in all—stories within stories. I keep the Russian doll on my desk to remind my patients and me that we all contain secret selves, and that therapy is a way to make contact with them.

Certainly, that was the journey Amelia and I took, and each step of it deepened her connection to the unknown parts of herself. It wasn't an easy journey or a direct one; along the way, serendipity played its part by way of the fire, and my therapist friend who introduced me to EMDR. The mystics knew that an untold number of variables interact to influence how our days will unfold. And as a therapist, I know that to find our inner selves, our own stories, and the stories within them, we need a few precious ingredients: time, patience, and a commitment to the process.

Recommended Reading

Eating Disorders

Andersen, Arnold. *Males with Eating Disorders*. New York: Brunner/ Mazel, 1990.

Andersen, Arnold; Leigh Cohn; and Thomas Holbrook. *Making Weight: Healing Men's Conflicts with Food, Weight and Shape*. Carlsbad, CA: Gürze Books, 2000.

Bloom, Carol; Andrea Gitter; Susan Gutwell; Laura Kogel; and Lela Zaphiropoulos. *Eating Problems: A Feminist Psychoanalytic Treatment Model*. New York: Basic Books, 1994.

Bruch, Hilde. *Eating Disorders: Obesity, Anorexia and the Person Within*. New York: Basic Books, 1973.

————. *The Golden Cage: The Enigma of Anorexia Nervosa*. Cambridge, MA: Harvard University Press, 1978.

Costin, Carolyn. *The Eating Disorder Sourcebook*. Los Angeles, CA: Lowell House, 1996.

————. *Your Dieting Daughter*. New York: Brunner/Mazel, 1996.

Fallon, Patricia; Melanie Katzman; and Susan Wooley, eds. *Feminist Perspectives on Eating Disorders*. New York: Guilford Press, 1993.

Garner, David M., and Paul E. Garfinkel, eds. *Handbook of Treatment for Eating Disorders*. New York: Guilford Press, 1997.

Hall, Lindsey, and Leigh Cohn. *Bulimia: A Guide to Recovery*. Carlsbad, CA: Gürze Books, 1999.

Hall, Lindsey, and Monika Ostroff. *Anorexia Nervosa: A Guide to Recovery*. Carlsbad, CA: Gürze Books, 1999.

Hall, Lindsey. *Full Lives*. Carlsbad, CA: Gürze Books, 1992.

Hirschmann, Jane, and Carol Munter. *When Women Stop Hating Their Bodies*. New York: Fawcett, 1995.

Hornyak, Lynn M., and Ellen K. Baker, eds. *Experiential Therapies for Eating Disorders*. New York: Guilford Press, 1991.

Johnson, Craig, ed. *Psychodynamic Treatment of Anorexia Nervosa and Bulimia*. New York: Guilford Press, 1991.

Johnston, Anita. *Eating in the Light of the Moon*. Carlsbad, CA: Gürze Books, 1996.

Kinoy, Barbara P., ed. *Eating Disorders: New Directions in Treatment and Recovery*. New York: Columbia University Press, 1994.

Levenkron, Steven. *The Best Little Girl in the World*. New York: Warner Books, 1981.

Orbach, Susie. *Fat is a Feminist Issue*. New York: Berkley Books, 1978.

———. *Fat is a Feminist Issue, II*. New York: Berkley Books, 1982.

Pennybaker, James W., ed. *Opening Up: The Healing Power of Expressing Emotions*. New York: Guilford Press, 1990.

Piran, Niva; Michael P. Levine; and Catherine Steiner-Adair. *Preventing Eating Disordes: A Handbook of Interventions and Special Challenges*. Philadelphia, PA: Brunner/Mazel, 1999.

Roth, Geneen. *When Food is Love: Exploring the Relationship between Eating and Intimacy*. New York: Plume Books, 1991.

Siegel, Michelle; Judith Brisman; and Margot Weinshel. *Surviving an Eating Disorder: Strategies For Family and Friends*. New York: Harper Perennial, 1997.

Werne, Joellen, and Irvin Yalom, eds. *Treating Eating Disorders*. San Francisco: Jossey-Bass, 1996.

Zerbe, Kathryn. *The Body Betrayed: A Deeper Understanding of Women, Eating Disorders and Treatment*. Carlsbad, CA: Gürze Books, 1993.

Family & Women's Issues

Bassoff, Evelyn. *Mothering Ourselves*. New York: Plume Press, 1991.

Brown, Lyn Mikel, and Carol Gilligan. *Meeting at the Crossroads: Women's Psychology and Girls' Development*. Cambridge, MA: Harvard University Press, 1992.

Caplan, Paula J. *The New Don't Blame Mother: Mending the Mother-Daughter Relationship*. Philadelphia, PA: Routledge, 2000.

Chernin, Kim. *The Obsession: Reflections on the Tyranny of Slenderness*. New York: Harper & Row, 1981.

Laidlaw, Toni Ann; Cheryl Malmo and Associates. *Healing Voices: Feminist Approaches to Therapy with Women*. San Francisco: Jossey-Bass, 1990.

Lerner, Harriet. *The Dance of Anger: A Woman's Guide to Changing the Patterns of Intimate Relationships*. New York: Harper & Row, 1986.

———. *The Dance of Intimacy*. New York: Harper & Row, 1989.

Maine, Margo. *Father Hunger: Fathers, Daughters and Food*. Carlsbad, CA: Gürze Books, 1991.

Pipher, Mary. *Reviving Ophelia*. New York: Ballantine Books, 1994.

Rogers, Annie, and Deborah Tolman, eds. *Women, Girls and Psychotherapy: Reframing Resistance*. New York: Harper Park Press, 1991.

Taffel, Ron, and Melinda Blau. *Second Famliy: How Adolescent Power Is Challenging the American Family*. New York: St. Martin's Press, 2001.

Wolf, Naomi. *The Beauty Myth*. New York: William Morrow, 1991.

———. *Fire with Fire: The New Female Power and How to Use It*. New York: Fawcett, 1994.

Relational Perspective of the Stone Center

Jordan, Judith, ed. *Women's Growth in Diversity*. New York: Guilford Press, 1997.

Jordan, Judith; Alexandra Kaplan; Jean Baker Miller; Irene Stiver; and Janet Surrey. *Women's Growth in Connection: Writings from the Stone Center*. New York: Guilford Press, 1991.

Miller, Jean Baker. *Towards a New Psychology of Women*. Boston: Beacon Press, 1976.

Miller, Jean Baker, and Irene Stiver. *The Healing Connection*. Boston: Beacon Press, 1997.

Guided Imagery

Hutchinson, Marcia. *Transforming Body Image: Love the Body You Have*. Watsonville, CA: Crossing Press, 1985.
Kearney-Cooke, Ann. "Reclaiming the Body: Using guided imagery in the treatment of body image disturbance among bulimic women." In Lynn M. Hornyak and Ellen K. Baker, eds. *Experiential Therapies for Eating Disorders*. New York: Guilford Press, 1991.

Journal Writing

Baldwin, Christine. *Journal Writing as a Spiritual Quest*. New York: Bantam, 1991.
Goldberg, Natalie. *Writing Down the Bones: Freeing the Writer Within*. Boston, MA: Shambhala Publications, 1986.
Metzger, Deena. *Writing for Your Life: A Guide and Companion to the Inner World*. San Francisco: Harper, 1992.

EMDR

Parnell, Laurel. *Transforming Trauma: EMDR*. New York: W.W. Norton & Company, 1997.
Shapiro, Francine, and Margot Silk Forest. *EMDR: The Breakthrough: Eye Movement Therapy for Overcoming Anxiety, Stress and Trauma*. New York: Basic Books, 1997.

Incest and Sexual Abuse

Bass, Ellen, and Laura Davis. *The Courage to Heal: A Guide for Women Survivors of Childhood Sexual Abuse*. New York: Harper & Row, 1988.
Cortois, Christine. *Healing the Incest Wound: Adult Survivors in Therapy*. New York: Norton Press, 1996.
Davis, Jodie, and Mary Gail Frawley. *Treating the Adult Survivor of Childhood Sexual Abuse*. New York: Basic Books, 1994.

Obsessive-Compulsive Disorder

Neziroglu, Fugen A., and Jose A. Yaryura-Tobias. *Over and Over Again: Understanding Obsessive-Compulsive Disorder*. New York: Lexington Books, 1995.

Rapoport, Judith. *The Boy Who Couldn't Stop Washing: The Experience and Treatment of Obsessive-Compulsive Disorder*. New York: Plume, 1990.

Self-Mutilation

Conterio, Karen; Wendy Lader; and Kingston Bloom. *Bodily Harm*. New York: Hyperion, 1999.

Farber, Sharon. *When the Body Is the Target: Self-Harm, Pain, and Traumatic Attachments*. New York: Jason Aronson, 2000.

Levenkron, Steven. *Cutting: Understanding and Overcoming Self-Mutilation*. New York: W.W. Norton, 1998.

Miller, Dusty. *Women Who Hurt Themselves: A Book of Hope and Understanding*. New York: Basic Books, 1994.

Trauma

Herman, Judith. *Trauma and Recovery*. New York: Basic Books, 1997.

Terr, Lenore. *Too Scared to Cry: Psychic Trauma in Childhood*. New York: HarperCollins, 1992.

van der Kolk, Bessel A; Alexander C. McFarlane; and Lars Weisaeth, eds. *Traumatic Stress: The Effects of Overwhelming Experience on Mind, Body and Society*. New York: Guilford Press, 1996.

Spirituality

Bilich, Marion; Susan Bonfiglio; and Steven Carlson. *Shared Grace: Therapists and Clergy Working Together*. Binghamton, NY: Haworth Press, 2000.

Cooper, David. *God Is a Verb: Kabbalah and the Practice of Mystical Judiasm*. New York: Riverhead Books, 1997.

Welwood, John, ed. *Ordinary Magic: Everyday Life as Spiritual Path*. Boston: Shambhala Publications, 1992.

Index

About the Author

Judith Ruskay Rabinor is the Director of The American Eating Disorders Center of Long Island, a Consultant to the Renfrew Center Foundation, an Associate Professor at the Derner Institute, Adelphi University in Garden City, New York, and editor of "The Therapist's Voice" column in *Eating Disorders: The Journal of Treatment and Prevention*. She is a noted lecturer, conducts workshops and training seminars, and has a private practice in Manhattan and Lido Beach, New York. Contact her or learn more about her workshop schedule at www.astarvingmadness.com.

About the Publisher

Since 1980, Gürze Books has specialized in quality information on eating disorders recovery, research, education, advocacy, and prevention. Gürze publishes books in this field, as well as the *Eating Disorders Review*, a clinical newsletter for professionals. They also widely distribute free copies of *The Eating Disorders Resource Catalogue*, which includes listings of books, tapes, and other information. Their website (www.bulimia.com) is an excellent internet gateway to treatment facilities, associations, basic facts, and other eating disorders sites.

Order Form

A *Starving Madness* is available at bookstores and libraries or may be ordered directly from Gürze Books.

FREE Catalogue

The Eating Disorders Resource Catalogue has more than 125 books on eating disorders and related topics, including body image, size-acceptance, self-esteem, and more. It is a valuable resource that includes listings of non-profit associations and treatment facilities, and it is handed out by therapists, educators, and other health care professionals throughout the world. Additional resources are also available at *www.bulimia.com*.

___ FREE copies of the *Eating Disorders Resource Catalogue*.

___ copies of A *Starving Madness*
   $14.95 per copy plus $2.90 each for shipping.

   Quantity discounts are available.

Name _____

Address _____

City, St, Zip _____

Phone _____

Gürze Books
P.O. Box 2238
Carlsbad, CA 92018
(800) 756-7533
www.bulimia.com